Sports Afloat

Other Publications:

THE ENCYCLOPEDIA OF COLLECTIBLES
WORLD WAR II
THE GREAT CITIES
HOME REPAIR AND IMPROVEMENT
THE WORLD'S WILD PLACES
HUMAN BEHAVIOR
THE ART OF SEWING
THE OLD WEST
THE EMERGENCE OF MAN
THE AMERICAN WILDERNESS
THE TIME-LIFE ENCYCLOPEDIA OF GARDENING
LIFE LIBRARY OF PHOTOGRAPHY
THIS FABULOUS CENTURY
FOODS OF THE WORLD
TIME-LIFE LIBRARY OF AMERICA
TIME-LIFE LIBRARY OF ART
GREAT AGES OF MAN
LIFE SCIENCE LIBRARY
THE LIFE HISTORY OF THE UNITED STATES
TIME READING PROGRAM
LIFE NATURE LIBRARY
LIFE WORLD LIBRARY
FAMILY LIBRARY:
    HOW THINGS WORK IN YOUR HOME
    THE TIME-LIFE BOOK OF THE FAMILY CAR
    THE TIME-LIFE FAMILY LEGAL GUIDE
    THE TIME-LIFE BOOK OF FAMILY FINANCE

Sports Afloat

By the Editors of
TIME-LIFE BOOKS

The
TIME-LIFE Library of Boating

TIME-LIFE BOOKS/ALEXANDRIA, VIRGINIA

The TIME-LIFE Library of Boating

The Cover: A 45-foot sport fisherman kicks up a low curtain of spume as it heads out from Port Everglades, Florida, to troll for sailfish in the Gulf Stream. The skipper steers from a control station on the bridge, while above him rises the light but sturdy structure of the boat's tuna tower.

The Consultants: David Beach is a fellow of the Royal Institution of Naval Architects and a member of the Society of Naval Architects and Marine Engineers. He has written numerous articles on boat design for the leading boating periodicals.

Jay Evans, director of recreational athletics at Hampshire College in Amherst, Massachusetts, coached the United States Olympic kayaking team in 1972.

Thomas C. Hardman serves as editor and publisher of the American Water Ski Association journal, *The Water Skier,* and is an authority on modern competitive water-skiing.

Frank T. Moss is an associate editor of *Yachting* magazine, editor of *Boat Owners Buyers Guide* and editor emeritus of *Sportfishing* magazine. He has also written two books on inland and offshore sport fishing.

William Munro, a representative for *Yachting* magazine, is a powerboatman with more than 30 years of experience. His photographs and articles have appeared in most of the major boating and fishing periodicals.

John Rousmaniere, a small-boat sailor and veteran ocean racer, is an associate editor at *Yachting* magazine.

John Urban, the author of the Appalachian Mountain Club's *White Water Handbook,* has canoed on eastern rivers for more than 20 years.

Correspondents: Elisabeth Kraemer (Bonn); Margot Hapgood, Dorothy Bacon (London); Susan Jonas, Lucy T. Voulgaris (New York); Maria Vincenza Aloisi, Josephine du Brusle (Paris); Ann Natanson (Rome). Valuable assistance was also provided by Carolyn T. Chubet (New York).

Contents

The Singular Excitement of Water Sports

The Singular Excitement of Water Sports

by Jim Harrison

The Leelanau Peninsula, where I live on a small farm, juts some 40 miles into northern Lake Michigan. On certain hilltops on the crown of land that forms the geologic spine of the peninsula, you can see water on three sides. Some eight years ago, after an extended stay in New York, I arrived on the peninsula at dawn after driving straight through. Cresting a hill, I spotted the old stone farmhouse. But beside it lay something far more splendid—the glint of water in the dawn sun. At the foot of a sloping two-mile hill stretched the 16-mile length of Lake Leelanau. Then came another long crest of hills with the pastel greens of late spring deepening into the darker greens of June, and beyond that the blue, glittering expanse of Lake Michigan.

There is an excitement to water, and to the multitude of enjoyments it offers, that strikes a deep, resonant chord in all of us. Perhaps it is the sense of freedom in venturing out into what Ernest Hemingway called the last wild country, a tractless world of our own, in which each of us can plunge into whatever activity or adventure he pleases. For some people this means skimming across the surface on a pair of water skis in the wake of a towboat at 35 miles an hour. To others, it is sliding down a back-country creek in a canoe, with no sound but the dip of the paddle into the stream and the breeze swaying the evergreen branches overhead. To a man in a kayak, it is the rush of adrenaline that comes as he plunges into the waterspouts, souse holes and standing waves of a white-water rapid. For the lithe and athletic, the excitement comes from skylarking about a harbor on a contraption called a Windsurfer, which is a kind of surfboard equipped with a bedsheet-sized sail. Or for some fanatical souls, it arrives with winter, when the lake freezes over and they can go clattering across its hardened surface in iceboats at more than a mile a minute.

To me, water means a chance to go fishing.

That morning, on my arrival home, I went over my fishing tackle. Then I spent the rest of the day driving around the country visiting the different marinas to check out the action. Every one was chockablock full of boats of every size and description. There were outriggered sport fishermen, humble 14-foot aluminum rowing dinghies and 70-foot cabin cruisers that had made the voyage all the way up from Florida. Some of their owners undoubtedly were readying their craft for one of the weekend salmon tournaments that take place all summer long in the small towns along the northeast coast of Lake Michigan. The fish that they pursue are the coho, which runs up to 30 pounds, and the Chinook, or king, salmon that reaches 60. Both of these varieties are pretty tough fighting fish while still green—a local Michigan term that means mature but still prespawning.

One attraction of the tournaments, to be sure, is the chance of hooking a cash prize of as much as $2,600, but the real reason most people go is the opportunity to mix with a host of other anglers in good water. In the old days before the Michigan Department of Natural Resources installed a dozen or so launching ramps in the area, trailerborne boats used to be lined up at tournament time for five miles back of the only launching site. I have commonly seen a couple of thousand boats churning out of the harbors at the height of the tournament season—some of them bona fide entrants, but most just ordinary people going out for a day's fishing. There are craft under 14 feet, really too small for safety, and 52-foot, $300,000 Hatteras cruisers. Once clear of the harbor they spread over a 10-by-15-mile stretch of water, exchanging information—and sometimes deliberate and artful misinformation—on their ship-to-shore radios. From the air the scene resembles some sort of comic armada, with a jangle of tangled lines and very bad tempers in the hot spots.

My own lifelong love affair with fishing—and with boats and water—began when I was still a kid, barely out of short pants. I remember standing in a barn with my father, who was the county agricultural agent in Michigan's Osceola County. A farmer was building us a rowboat out of white pine, and I smelled the resinous wood shavings that littered the hay chaff and watched the barn swallows dart around the rafters and ropes and hay pulleys. The half-built boat was a total mystery to a nine-year-old, but nonetheless an exciting promise of vague future delights.

The future began to take more real shape with the delivery of the completed craft at the small lake where my father and his brothers had built the cabin in which we spent our summers. We watched the launching of that heavy, cumbersome skiff, splendid in its fresh gray paint, as if it had been an ocean liner sliding down the bank to float among the lily pads. It had cost the sum of $50, and my brother and I cleansed and cared for it as religiously as if it had cost $50,000. We would wait in frantic competition to be chosen to row my father or mother around the lake in the evening to plug for bass. Some of my happiest memories are bound up with the creak of oars, the cries of herons and loons, the plop of the bass plug on the water, and the hiss of the kerosene lantern, whose mellow glow encircled the delicious aroma of a late-night fish fry. It was years before it occurred to me that being given the honor of cleaning all the fish, or of rowing my Swedish-farmer grandfather around the lake for up to 12 hours at a stretch, was really more in the nature of being a chore than a high privilege.

It has also dawned upon me belatedly that, in its humble way, that first rowboat was the beginning of real knowledge of the water, and of how to move on it. In that boat, my father taught me to row, and to tack in zigzags into the waves rather than to roll sloppily into the troughs. I also learned that driving a boat is not like driving a car. There is far less margin of safety. You don't just pull up to a dock and put on the brakes. And when you start to turn a rowboat, you go sideways for a while. You have to think about all these maneuvers in advance, and you have to really understand them before you ever get into your first powerboat.

I also began to appreciate that easily half of the success of any boatborne fisherman is due to the skill of the boat handler. Some 30 years after that first rowboat took possession of my soul, I was fighting a big fish—a striped marlin by the feel of it—in the confluence of the Humboldt and El Niño currents 20 miles off the coast of Ecuador. I was an hour into the fish, and the equatorial heat had pushed me toward terminal fatigue. Worse yet, I was working from a dead boat. Our single engine had quit, and the captain was unable to help me by moving the boat slowly forward to help raise the fish or by making the long, sweeping curves that would temporarily create less tension in the line so that I could take it in. (Such maneuvers had been worked out years before by pioneer deep-sea fishermen like Zane Grey. Once Grey battled for nine hours to bring in a swordfish he had hooked, and then discovered that all that time he had been mostly fighting the tension on his own line while the swordfish had been feeding.) My fish sounded. Without getting any help from the boat, it is almost impossible to haul up from the depths a big fish that is sulking, or one that has died from too rapid a change in water pressure. I was afraid that I'd lost him.

We drifted on the swells in a silence broken only by the soft fluffing sound of the wings of the frigate birds and the staccato Spanish of the mates. We had no radio and no other boat was in sight, not even one of those small skiffs in which Peruvian fishermen venture out to purse seine for small fish. I felt like a boxer nearing the end of a club fight in which his opponent is the referee's brother. My imagination called up visions of a watery demise among the venomous yellow sea snakes that were drifting here and there around us. But after a seemingly endless hour of hammering and tinkering, the captain got the engine started again. And by expertly maneuvering the boat, he helped me to bring up the fish—which proved to be not a marlin but another fine trophy, a 190-pound sailfish.

Fishing the flats off Florida for tarpon and bonefish demands a somewhat

Author Jim Harrison, wielding the pole of a lone fishing boat in the Florida Keys, has been zestfully involved with water sports for more than 30 years. A frequent contributor of articles on fishing and the outdoors to Sports Illustrated and other magazines, he has also published four volumes of poetry and three novels. In the intervals, he has plied his fishing rod from Canada to Ecuador.

different but no less exacting kind of skill, one that nobody practices more deftly than a Florida Keys tarpon guide I know, who fishes out of Little Torch Key. His touch is apparent just in the way that he drives his bonefish skiff to the fishing grounds. An ordinary boatman heads straight for his objective as fast as an 85- to 135-horsepower outboard will push the low-profiled craft; on a rough day, his passenger is apt to arrive soaking wet. My friend zigzags among the keys, plotting his course to keep in the lee of one island after another. He may take an extra 15 minutes, but the fisherman stays dry.

More marvelous still is to watch him pole a boat. He is a former U.S. Navy physical-training instructor, and he can probably still press 150 pounds. He can pole that boat upwind or uptide, and he can make it go so fast it leaves a wake. But strength is only part of the marvel. To turn a boat while poling, an amateur like me has to twist his body. But my friend does it just by planting the pole exactly where he wants it—to the rear or to one side—with the timing of a pole vaulter, but with greater skill, since he makes his plant behind him, and by touch rather than by sight. He can pole that shallow-draft boat in a dew, as they say in the trade, and so quietly that the spookiest of fish will never hear him coming.

Boat-handling abilities like this are one reason that guides are not allowed to post international game-fish records. If they were, they would hold them all. This particular guide recently caught a tarpon that was about 50 pounds over the salt-water fly-fishing record—and, being a staunch conservationist, promptly threw it back.

At the exact opposite end of the scale in maneuverability from a bonefish skiff is the craft I use for duckhunting on Lake Okeechobee. This is a large truck inner tube with a sling for a seat. It is unbelievably awkward, especially when you have a 70-pound Labrador retriever sitting in your lap. You cover yourself with camouflage cloth and wait for the ducks. The recoil of your gun sends you spinning in half circles. During slow periods you keep an eye out for alligators. A big one snuck up uncomfortably close one day and stole half our ducks. My rage over the loss was tempered by relief that the alligator had preferred the ducks to one—or both—of the legs that I was trolling so vulnerably in the water.

For fishing backwoods lakes and rivers that are virtually unreachable overland, I favor a johnboat or a canoe. A johnboat, flat and boxy, is roomier and infinitely more comfortable to fish from than a canoe. But it is less maneuverable and far more apt to slide out from under you when you stand up on the seat to cast. This happened to me one day when I was fishing around a logjam. Most Michigan rivers have eddies where fallen trees and branches and old saw logs have been gathering into a big knot for who knows how long. White-pine logs, so big that they might have been felled 100 years ago when most of the real giants were cut, have been washed out of some of these jams by storms. When dried out and sawed up, they are still perfectly usable. A jam is a prime trout habitat; a brown trout that is seeking food and shelter might take a station there for life.

I was trying for one of these settlers when the boat took a weird little turn and I fell into the logjam, catching my jacket on a branch in a way that held me pinned under water. The boat handler can't do much in such a situation except stop the boat—which may take a while in a stiff current. What saved me was the experience of having often gone under in my waders. If you relax when that happens, the river will eventually carry you into an eddy and you can get out. If you thrash about in wild-eyed panic, you can expend so much energy that you move into shock, and if the water is cold, you are subject to hypothermia, a sometimes fatal lowering of your body temperature. I held my breath and with calm deliberation wriggled around until I could unhook the jacket and scramble onto a log.

Barring such occasional accidents, johnboats make eminently sensible backwoods fishing craft. But to me, there is one kind of craft that goes beyond the sensible, a boat that is part magic.

Something about a canoe makes it esthetically unmatchable—particularly the old-fashioned wood-and-canvas type. It melds better into a wilderness setting than a silver aluminum johnboat. I think a universal desire to play Indian is part of it. Like thousands of other northern-Michigan youngsters, I destroyed half a dozen birch trees in my youth trying to build a canoe of bark. Hardly anyone paddles·around in birchbark, of course, and for my money no vessel on earth compares in grace, beauty and good handling qualities with, say, a 15-foot wood-and-canvas job. It weighs only 58 pounds, and you can get a sense of ease and maneuverability out of it. And it is quiet. While drifting along through cedar swamps, the quietness of a canoe has allowed me to see innumerable ducks, beaver and deer, nesting eagles, and once a bobcat that came down to the water to drink. Bobcats are primarily nocturnal creatures; you almost never see one by daylight, but a canoe is a passport even to a bobcat's world.

The canoe—as well as its Eskimo brother the kayak—is also a passport to white-water running, a form of sport that scares the hell out of me. On some western rivers—the middle branch of the Salmon in Idaho, say, or parts of the Yellowstone in Montana—the roar of the water sounds like a freight train. A friend of mine who floated down the Salmon a couple of years ago during the spring runoff says he came around a corner and there, suddenly, was a wave that he _knew_ was 40 feet high billowing back from the canyon wall. The physics of that are preposterous.

I would sooner trust my luck in a kayak on an Alaskan river, however, than in one of the iceboats I sometimes see flitting along Lake Leelanau on an arctic afternoon. Those of my friends who enjoy the sport tell me it's worth the weeks of watching the weather, the logistical problems involved in rounding up all the other fanatics at a moment's notice when ice and wind are right, the trouble of trekking miles to the nearest available site, and the bother of bundling up in snowsuits that conceal all evidence of age or sex. My own view is that ice belongs in drinks and I belong somewhere other than perched on a fence rail going 100 miles an hour at 20 below zero. I must admit, though, that it looks like the thrill of a lifetime.

Water-skiing appears to the uninitiated to be even more precarious than iceboating, but with a skilled driver at the helm it can be safer than most downhill runs on snow. With an idiot at the helm, it can be something close to suicide. Ask my brother. He and I took up water-skiing on that same lake where we had learned to row. With unbounded and baseless confidence, we set out in a light but sturdy outboard that our family had lately acquired. I took the helm first and, after a few false starts, got my brother up on top of the water. We were soon roaring around the lake, close enough to the shore so that anybody who happened to be about could admire our skill. I was looking back over my shoulder at my brother who was skiing so close behind the boat that I could read his ecstatic expression. He was, in fact, far too close to the boat. Our hastily chosen towrope was about half the length that it should have been. Suddenly his face registered incredulous dismay. A second later the boat was plowing right through a flimsy wooden dock. Still clinging reflexively to the towrope and leaning back to avoid the flying debris, my brother shot through the path the boat had cleared. On the other side, I cut the motor and we drifted to a stop amid floating remnants of the demolished dock. The boat was intact except for some scratched paint, and our injuries were chiefly to our pride.

But mishaps are the exception in water sports. For the most part, whether you are lazing on a converted lobster boat off Halibut Point near Gloucester, Massachusetts, or casting for brown trout from a johnboat on the Yellowstone, it is all fine. The water is there and we can all own it and there are few reasons to get upset—literally or figuratively. The beauty, the fun, the slight spice of danger in sports afloat offset the troubles, the hardships, the fears. And rightly so, or else we would stay safely tucked in our living rooms with small chance for happiness.

1 More than 75 per cent of all pleasure boats operated in the United States today are used at least part time for fishing. On them, 30 million people pursue fish of all descriptions on rivers, lakes and seas, in boats of all shapes and sizes: one-man rubber rafts that can be deflated and backpacked, 14-ton deep-sea game-fishing cruisers like the one at left, skiffs that double as water-ski boats or family-outing launches, and highly specialized craft for stalking the wary bonefish on the Florida sand flats. Within this armada of seven million craft, those best suited for fishing bear certain family resemblances. They give fast and reliable transportation to and from fishing sites, provide a reasonably secure platform from

THE FAMILY OF FISHING BOATS

which to fish, and have spacious, open hulls or roomy, uncluttered cockpits with maximum working room. Cunningly contrived lockers, wells and ice chests allow plenty of safe, convenient stowage space for tackle and bait —and for bringing back the catch, dead or alive. Deck hardware and any other topside obstructions that might ensnare a fishing line are either eliminated entirely or tucked away.

Amazingly enough, such conveniences have been available to most devotees of America's number-one outdoor sport only in the past three or four decades. In the first quarter of the century, sport-fishing boats, both seagoing and those for inland waters, were for the most part short-range, slow or clumsy —or all three. Then, in the late 1920s, with the advent of reliable marine engines, fishing boats began quickly to evolve toward the agile, totally utilitarian sports craft of today. The first efficient, mass-produced outboards, 2- to 3½-horsepower units that eliminated the back-wrenching chore of rowing, were eagerly adopted by small-boat fishermen. At about the same time, innovative deep-sea anglers began to acquire vessels that could go far and fast in search of tuna, swordfish, sailfish and marlin.

Among the first boats to be adapted for sport fishing were a handful of 35- to 40-foot, 100-horsepower World War I torpedo retrievers, which could be picked up for $500 to $1,000 in the early Depression years. They were followed, after the repeal of Prohibition, by converted rumrunners, sleek craft with light, efficient hulls powered by truck or tractor motors. Seeking more efficient ways of battling big game fish aboard these better craft, early sport-fishing enthusiasts installed office-type swivel chairs in their cockpits. To deploy as many lines as possible over the greatest possible area, they lashed bamboo poles to their cabin trunks, and to provide a better view of fish and baits, they jury-rigged steering stations atop cabins. One ingenious skipper contrived a crow's-nest by erecting a sawed-off mast from an old schooner. From these primitive improvisations emerged such highly sophisticated equipment as the fighting chair on pages 38-39, aluminum or fiberglass outriggers, and strong, lightweight aluminum tuna towers.

At first, these refinements were turned out only by one or two pioneering custom boatyards—the best of which continue to build exquisitely handcrafted deep-sea fishing vessels at the rate of three or four a year. By 1960, however, mass builders began producing sport-fishing craft by the flotilla. And as they did so, the elaborate technology that was developed for these larger boats started to filter down to the makers and modifiers of smaller boats, both in the backyard and in the factory. Modern small-craft modifications, whether they are done at home or commercially, may be as extensive as the complete customizing of a bass boat, such as the one on pages 18 and 19, or as simple as the lashing down of a bait-cutting board onto an inflatable backpacker's raft *(page 15)*. Either way, the capability of the boat is enhanced—and so is the owner's chance to catch a fish.

From the flying bridge of a 45-foot cruiser, a sport-fishing skipper watches a lure dancing just below the surface, while a crewman in the tuna tower scans the sea for feeding fish.

Convenient Cartoppers

The boats pictured here and on the opposite page are typical of the very simplest craft favored by lake and river fishermen. Their popularity is easy to understand. All of them can be transported on a cartop anywhere the car can go, hand-carried from the car to lake- or streamside, and launched even in the absence of a ramp. Inflatable boats like the one shown at lower left on the opposite page can even be backpacked to wilderness lakes whose best fishing holes would otherwise be totally unreachable.

Noninflatable cartoppers average between 85 and 160 pounds in weight—light enough for two adults to swing onto or lift down from the roof of an automobile and to carry or drag a reasonable distance to water. Inflatables may weigh as little as 12 pounds—oars, air pump and all.

An angler of average strength and coordination can row, paddle or pole any of these boats, and all—including the inflatable—can be fitted with small outboards for faster running to fishing sites or for trolling after arrival.

With the natural exception of the inflatables, all of these cartoppers were originally made of wood—as the dory-styled McKenzie riverboat at top right still is. Fiberglass and aluminum, however, have largely replaced wood in modern canoes, johnboats and skiffs. Each material has its advantages. Aluminum boats are the lightest and, pound for pound, strongest. But they are also the noisiest—a drawback when approaching easily alarmed fish. Their thin metal hulls act as resonators and amplify the sound of the motor, the shuffling of feet on the bilge or even waves slapping against the side. Fiberglass, though heavier, is less rackety—and wood is heaviest and quietest of all.

The square-ended aluminum johnboat (above) is the descendant of small, homemade 19th Century barges designed to carry maximum cargo on one-way downriver trips—at the end of which both boat and cargo were sold. Of all cartoppers it still offers the boatman the most space for his money. Its flat bottom and shallow draft make it easy to propel and maneuver. The johnboat tends to rock and pound in choppy waters and, when it is under power, to skid on sharp turns. But for leisurely fishing in protected waters, it has few equals.

The trout fishermen at left are drifting down Montana's Big Blackfoot River in a 12-foot version of the wooden McKenzie riverboat. This modern miniature of the woodsman's old double-ender is squared off at the stern for outboard power when needed. Though weighing only 160 pounds, it is a steady craft for turbulent streams, and its hull can withstand severe poundings against rocky river bottoms.

The 15-foot square-transom canoe below is less stable than more conventional craft, but like all canoes (pages 86-107), it is light and maneuverable. A beamy 43 inches wide, it easily accommodates two anglers, their auxiliary paddles and fishing gear, plus food, duffel and the day's catch. Spray rails along the sides deflect waves; a one-inch keel adds strength and helps to hold the boat on course.

A compendium of the virtues needed in small fishing craft, this 12-foot aluminum modified-V-bottomed skiff is strong, light, stable and exceptionally seaworthy. It is easy to row, and can accommodate an outboard motor of up to 10 hp. When trolling under power, it rides well, handles smoothly and responds quickly to steering changes.

Inflatables like the one shown at left are by far the lightest of the boats pictured and, when deflated, are the most compact. They can navigate in a few inches of water, and though subject to punctures from sharp obstacles, they bounce easily off rocks that would dent aluminum, crack fiberglass or splinter wood. However, inflatables lack firm, flat surfaces, a disadvantage the owner of this craft has remedied by lashing a wooden platform athwart the boat's topsides.

A 15-foot Boston Whaler carries two fishermen who are casting into the rocks for striped bass over the slate-gray chop of the Atlantic Ocean off Newport, Rhode Island. A model of stability, the Whaler's essentially flat bottom has been given a slightly V-shaped forefoot to reduce slapping on head seas; pontoon-like sponsons on either side not only trap air to cushion rides on choppy water, but also keep the boat steady when an angler walks from one side to the other. High-density urethane foam fills the space between the hull's outer and inner fiberglass skins, giving Whalers extra buoyancy and strength.

Two anglers still-fish for sea trout from their 17-foot Boston Whaler in the placid waters near Charlotte Harbor off Stuart, Florida. The stainless-steel railings extending around three sides of the boat and on the bow help prevent the fishermen from slipping overboard. And to give them space to stand and move around, the forward portion of the cockpit is covered here by a removable wooden deck section.

Stable Runabouts

The two types of boats shown here—the Boston Whalers at left and the versatile runabout at right—are popular examples of utilitarian craft in the class of fishing boats just above the small cartoppers. Overall they measure in the 13- to 17-foot range; the smallest weigh 300 pounds and the largest 950; thus, they are easily trailered to fishing areas on inland lakes, rivers or in coastal waters. Originally designed as utility craft for either family day cruising, water-skiing or fishing, they have open, uncluttered cockpits that give elbow room for two- or three-man angling parties. The normal power plant for these craft is a 20- to 60-horsepower outboard engine that, fitted with six-gallon portable tanks, can provide a range of more than 30 miles.

Both types of boat are exceptionally stable, owing in part to their generous beam-to-length ratios of better than 3 to 1 —that is, a Whaler 15 feet long will have a beam of no less than five and one half feet. This ratio produces a wide platform hull that gives the fisherman stable footing, so he can stand up to cast with no danger of rocking the boat. And the steadiness of the runabout is such that even when the boat is underway the angler has no trouble making his casts.

The hull shapes also make the boats easy to handle, even during rough weather—an essential prerequisite for fishing craft. The high freeboard of the runabout tends to make it run dry, preventing spray from dousing the interiors. The Whaler, while it is just as seaworthy, has a slightly lower freeboard, which gives fishermen an easier task when it comes time to boat their catch.

A pair of fishermen stand in the cockpit of their 17-foot runabout while fishing for coho salmon in a British Columbia fjord. The modified-V bow and forward sections are designed to slice through rough waters, while the broad, flat after sections provide a steady platform for the fishermen. At top speed the 25-horsepower engine will push the boat at 30-mile-per-hour planing speeds, even with two big men aboard. For this kind of fast running, the permanent windshield deflects spray from the face of the skipper and crew.

Perched in a comfortable swivel chair at the forward end of the uncluttered deck, the compleat bass fisherman casts for fish while maneuvering his boat with the assistance of a tiny 12-volt electric trolling motor, shown in detail below. The control pedal beneath his right foot regulates speed and at the same time turns the motor to steer the boat. The low-slung craft is not only less disturbing to fish than conventional models but offers a minimum of wind resistance.

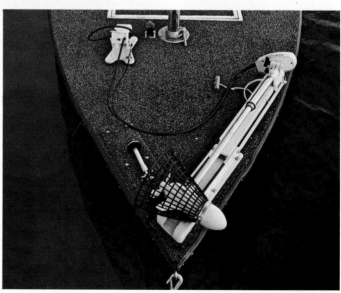

The trolling motor is shown stowed securely in its own permanently mounted bracket. When needed, it tips easily over the bow and locks into place. A basket-shaped guard around the five-inch propeller keeps the blades from hitting rocks or from becoming entangled in vegetation. The cord connecting the motor and its control pedal to a 12-volt battery under the stern deck plugs into a socket at the base of the forward chair.

A Customized Bass Boat

For years bass fishermen made do with unpretentious craft with the basic but humble virtues of being easy to propel on rivers and lakes, and reasonably comfortable for hours of casting or trolling. In the past decade, however, some highly specialized bass-hunting rigs have been developed. Some, like those on pages 78-85, are stock models; others are handcrafted conversions like the 17-foot fishing machine here. Its owner, who is a tournament-going angler from Florida, sliced 14 inches off its freeboard to make the boat's profile less visible to surface-swimming bass. Within the hull he built rod lockers, compartments for storing extra batteries and safety gear, a 12-gallon fuel tank, and wells with an aerating water system for keeping bait and catch alive. He laid indoor-outdoor carpeting over a flush plywood deck broken only by a small cockpit amidships, and installed swiveling pedestal seats for 360° casting.

A foot-controlled electric motor on the bow provides slow, silent propulsion at the fishing grounds, while leaving both of the angler's hands free to fish. And to save precious time during tournaments, a 135-horsepower outboard motor provides quick rides to distant holes.

The owner selects a rod from one of the twin rod lockers (1 and 2) that he has built into the boat on either side of the cockpit. Beneath the large hatch (3) behind the bow chair is an ice chest and one of the boat's two 15-gallon live-bait wells, connected by an aerated recirculating water system to an identical well (4) in the stern. The locker on the port side of the stern deck (5) is for stowing safety equipment, and the hatch next to it (6) provides access to the vessel's two 12-volt batteries. The fuel tank that supplies the big outboard is under the rear deck and fills through a small hatch (7).

Moving along after dark near Lake Okeechobee, the bass-boat skipper finds his way with the help of two 12-volt docking lights that he has installed in the bow. Designed for use on larger boats, the lights reach ahead like auto headlights and enable him to spot objects in his path at distances up to 750 feet. Heavy-duty mechanical steering gives him excellent control. His right hand grips the throttle lever, on which he has also mounted the trim buttons that adjust the angle of the motor to the transom; he can thus regulate both the boat's speed and its attitude while keeping his left hand on the wheel.

This customized bonefishing boat has a broad bow that provides a
spacious platform for the boat handler and houses a safety-equipment
locker, accessible through a hatch inside the cockpit (1). Walk-around
side decks (2 and 3) offer extra working area for the boat handler as
he plies his pole. Rod and gear lockers under the side decks (4 and 5)
contain approximately 16 square feet of stowage space. And hidden
beneath flush-mounted hatches in the stern casting platform are
an ice chest (6), an aerated bait well (7), a fuel tank (8), and a gear
locker (9). A 12-volt battery is under the steering console (10).

Built for the Shallows

In trying to catch bonefish in their favored feeding grounds, such as the shallow sand flats off Florida, half the battle is getting close enough to cast for the wary creatures without frightening them. The best bonefishermen do their stalking in boats of the type pictured here. Both are roomy, 18-foot open skiffs with space for two people and their gear. Most important is the shallow draft—only eight inches with the engine tilted up—that allows the boats to be poled within 30 feet of the feeding fish without stirring up a telltale cloud of sand. Low topsides also help give the craft a less visible profile.

There are two separate working areas on a typical bonefishing boat, each handled by one of two partners. The wide and decked-over bow provides a spacious platform on which the boat handler can wield his pole—as described on pages 98-99. A stern area is reserved for the person doing the fishing. In many boats, including those shown here, the platforms also serve as tops for lockers and live-bait wells. The remarkably uncluttered decks are particularly important for this type of angling, for a freshly hooked bonefish may race wildly in any direction for 50 to 100 yards at a stretch.

A Dividend of Silence and Safety

These flats fishermen have equipped their craft bow and stern with a removable deck covering of skid-resistant indoor-outdoor carpeting that makes for safer fishing and boat handling. Held by matching pairs of snaps sewn into the carpet and screwed into the boat's deck, the carpet provides greater traction underfoot for both the guide and the fisherman, and reduces noise that might frighten away the fish.

Holders for three fishing rods are conveniently located inside the eight-foot-long lockers on each side of the cockpit of the boat at left. The rubber safety cord that is strung vertically over the open brackets keeps the rods securely in their place in choppy seas.

Live shrimp for bait stay vigorous and healthy in this five-gallon bait well, which is filled with sea water through the faucet and then continuously aerated by a small, electrically run system similar to those used in home fish tanks. Four to five dozen average shrimp will easily last in the well for the duration of an eight-hour fishing trip.

Churning out into the Gulf of Mexico, a 23-footer with Bimini top raised against the sun spews foam from her 140-horsepower twin inboard-outboard engines. Besides the power plant, this model center-console boat differs from the one at right mainly in the addition of a cuddy cabin and head in the bow. Entered by a companionway hatch located forward of the console, the cabin provides spartan sleeping accommodations for two people; but it sharply reduces the space available for fishing. Nevertheless, a closed shelter is popular among some fishermen aboard these relatively small boats —not only for occasional overnighting, but as shelter from rain.

Center Consoles

Center-console fishing boats, like the two shown here, are favorites of anglers who ply coastal waters for game fish. With the wheel, electronic equipment and all operational controls placed neatly in the center, the way is cleared for around-the-boat fishing. Such open-console craft are only 17 to 28 feet long, but their excellent design makes them capable of pursuing fish as much as 50 to 60 miles offshore.

Though hull shapes differ according to the locale where the boats are generally fished, these two are descendants of the south Florida bay skiff, a broad, flat-hulled vessel that was originally developed to probe the expansive shallow reaches of Florida Bay. To improve handling qualities in a following sea, and to reduce pounding when heading into a chop, these modern center consoles have modified-V-shaped hulls. On both craft, the props can be raised to allow the boats to glide or be poled into waters barely two feet deep. Built-in fuel tanks deliver a cruising range of up to 200 miles, and both boats have enough power to make 30-knot runs home in a building sea.

A superbly efficient sports craft, this 22-foot center-console outboard is powered by twin 85-horsepower engines with gas tanks beneath the console. Around the wheel is an array of sophisticated electronic gear—depth and fish finder (1), control panel (2), and VHF-FM radio (3). Spinning-rod holders (4) are mounted on the console, as is a brace (5) for the fishing-kite reel. Demountable outriggers (6) are set on each gunwale, along with a series of rod holders (7). To keep fishing lines from snagging, the rear mooring cleats are inboard (8); a bow rail helps to keep such lines above the forward cleats and chocks (9).

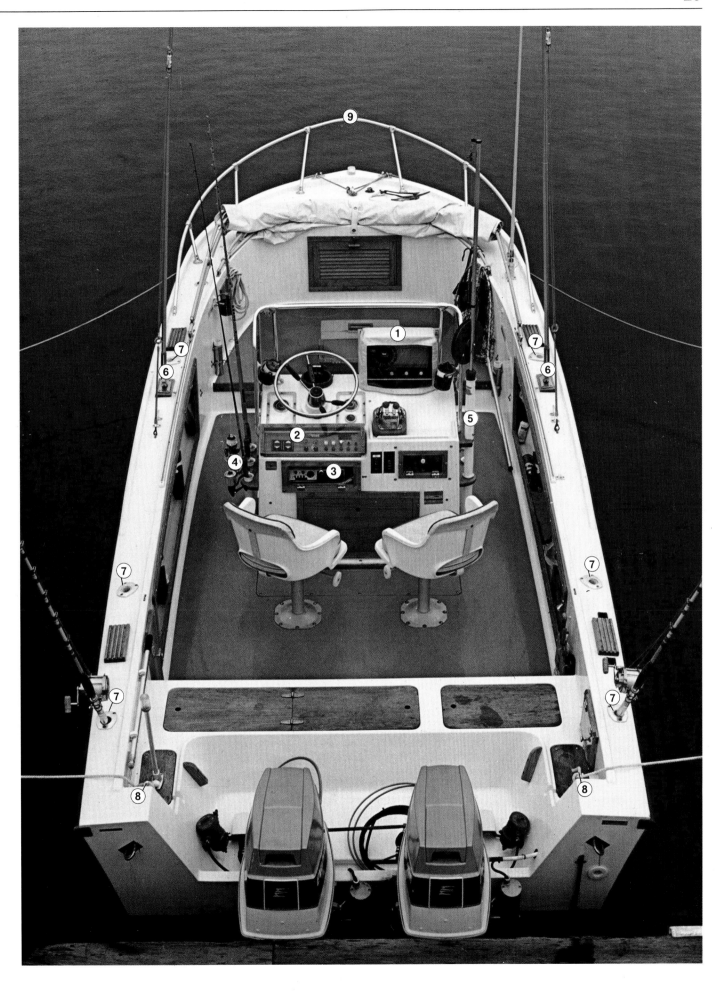

A soft-riding, spray-deflecting cathedral hull, a cuddy cabin and demountable outriggers make a versatile offshore fisherman of this 24-footer. Here the skipper is navigating comfortably and steadily through whitecaps in the choppy seas of the Gulf Stream between Bimini and Florida. The compact cabin contains a double berth, head, and stowage for duffel, life vests and extra rods.

Buoyant sponsons on either side of the narrow central hull provide the lateral stability of a beamy design with almost none of a wide boat's normal tendency to pound. Deep longitudinal slots between the sponsons and center hull create air cushions to soften the boat's entry into each succeeding wave, letting the craft clip along comfortably at planing speeds even on the open ocean.

The Cathedral Hull

A four-wheeled tilt-bed trailer permits the boat to be launched by one person, either from a paved ramp like the one below, or from a hard, sandy beach. The 11-by-6-foot cockpit contains the engine in a boxlike housing at the stern, a bait well, ice-and-fish chest, a fishing chair and twin chairs at the control console for skipper and crew. When retrailering at day's end, the skipper uses the trailer's battery-powered winch to haul the craft back onto the vehicle's bed.

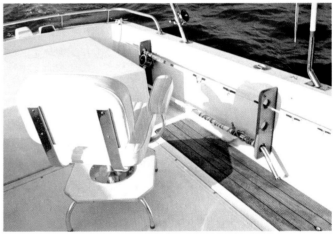

Built-in racks on the port (above) and starboard sides of the cockpit double as holders for rods and removable outriggers. The circular chrome collars in the deck above the racks receive the rod butts when lines are being trolled. A teak-covered recessed well below the racks holds live bait, and an identical well on the opposite side of the cockpit holds fish. Though most fishing chairs are bolted through the deck, the cathedral hull's inherent stability helps keep the movable fishing chair steady with only rubber collars on the legs.

A walk-around recessed deck enclosed by a grab rail gives the angler the mobility and safety he needs when a fighting fish decides to circle the boat. Ten inches wide and a foot below the gunwale level, the deck has a nonskid fiberglass surface for better traction.

*A modern version of the old Maine lobster boat glides through the
waters of Stuart, Florida. It has been given a canopied center console
(where the skipper stands), antennae for electronic gear, outriggers
for trolling, fishing chairs, and an anodized aluminum railing forward.
The blue cushion in front of the console covers the engine box; the
small cabin tucked up toward the bow has a head and bunks for two.*

Remodeled for Sport

In recent years more and more boatmen —fishermen included—have been drawn to the classic lines of old wooden boats, dressed up in modern materials and gear. One of the most ingenious of these is the adaptation shown here of the Maine lobster boat, which recently has made an appearance in sunny Florida.

More than nostalgia has reawakened interest in this boat; its design elements are supremely functional. The original model, made near Jonesport, Maine, in the late 1800s, had a high, sharp bow for cutting through rough coastal waters, a flat run aft for a good turn of speed with modest power, and low freeboard amidships for hauling in lobster pots. Its full, round bilge, generous beam and sharp forefoot made it seaworthy even on stormy nights. So effective was this design in piloting through Maine's choppy waters that latter-day models are still being turned out in small family boatyards down East.

With the substitution of fiberglass for wood, and other minor modifications —among them a slight V in the flat stern for better control in a following sea—the old Maine lobsterman has come to vigorous life as a vehicle for stalking marlin, dolphin and bonita in the Gulf Stream.

Viewed from astern, the nonskid 100-square-foot cockpit of the lobsterman glows in the Florida sun. The helmsman's chair is permanently swivel-mounted, and can function as a fishing chair; the other fishing chairs are portable. The teak side decks aft of the outriggers contain four round chrome rod holders, a pair of hawsepipes leading to cleats beneath, and three fuel fills.

The trim console standing amidships allows plenty of deck room for moving about. Radio, depth finders and other electronic gear are ingeniously tucked under the canvas-and-aluminum canopy, where they are not only sheltered from rain and spray, but also take advantage of space that usually is unused.

Compact Cruiser

To go after big game fish—sailfish, marlin, shark and other 150-plus pounders that swim in offshore waters—requires a full-fledged cruising boat. It must be well enough fitted out so that the angler and crew can live aboard for several days at a time. The boat must also be sufficiently seaworthy to make fast runs home in deteriorating weather, and nimble enough for quick maneuvering when a struggling fish is on the hook.

The compact offshore fisherman at left is just such a boat. Thirty-one feet overall, it is a relative baby among deepwater cruisers, which normally run from 35 to 60 feet and more. It is also eminently utilitarian. All its cockpit and topside gear are there for catching and landing fish. No space is wasted, no frivolous ornaments get in the way of tackle and lines. The cockpit is remarkably roomy (overleaf) to provide an arena for fighting the fish.

The flying bridge, from which the skipper operates the boat, is of special importance. From this elevated station the skipper can more readily find fish. From here he also gives the angler directions when it is time to strike. And then, as the fight goes on, he maneuvers the boat to give the angler the maximum advantage (pages 74-75), and to keep the fishing line clear of the boat's propeller.

Purposeful in each of its silhouetted details, a tightly designed offshore fisherman trolls in Florida waters. The tall vertical poles are antennae for electronic gear; diagonal ones are outriggers for trolling lines. Four rods rest in holders around the angler standing by the fighting chair, while the skipper steers from the flying bridge. Most often such boats have modified-V hulls for rough-water stability, and twin engines for maneuverability.

The rotating fighting chair—a complex and formidable instrument—faces the stern from its permanent mounting in the cockpit. Its movable back and its footrest can be adjusted to the fisherman's comfort and then locked into position. The footrest lets the angler brace his feet for leverage when he has hooked a big one. If several anglers are aboard, the one whose trolling line hooked the fish takes the chair; the others haul in the inactive lines while he wrestles the fish.

A big game angler checks one of his trolling lines in the stern of the uncluttered cockpit. A beam of 11 feet allows 110 square feet of open room for the angler and the fighting chair. The grab rail is an excellent safety feature for rough seas. Brackets for storing the gaff and other equipment are neatly secured underneath the gunwales, where they will not foul any lines, and the hatches are flush on the deck. The portable box astern holds iced bait for the trolling rods.

A canvas canopy shields the helmsman on the flying bridge from a blistering tropical sun, while wrap-around coverings over the cabin windows help keep the cabin cool. Despite its relatively small size, the cabin has another control station, a galley, dinette and berths for four persons—and a locker for storing fishing tackle.

See-through plastic screens, bordered in sturdy canvas, can be rolled up for fair-weather sailing, and lowered to give additional protection to the flying bridge, its helmsman and precious electronic gear.

The Ultimate Fisherman

Within the family of fishing boats, the ruling member is the king-sized offshore tournament cruiser. These superb craft, which range from 40 to 75 feet in length, contain virtually every kind of fishing gear found in other boats, but on a grander scale. The most elaborate of them are capable of traveling across oceans to seek out, fight and land salt-water game fish that may weigh over a thousand pounds each, and do so in any kind of weather. Along with these ultimate sporting capabilities, such boats provide the live-aboard luxury of a first-class yacht.

The imposing craft at right, incongruously christened "Little Pete," is the epitome of the tournament cruiser. Designed and built at the Rybovich Boat Yard in Florida, it took two and a half years to finish and was made entirely by hand from the bottom of its 58-foot glass-over-wood hull to the top of the 34-foot tuna tower.

Little Pete is powered by a pair of 595-horsepower engines backed by a 1,500-gallon fuel supply that allow the boat to cruise at 23 knots over a range of 750 miles. Whether cruising or trolling, the skipper can handle the boat from any of three separate steering stations: one in the tuna tower, one in the cockpit, and a third in the flying bridge—which is equipped with radio, radar, and other electronic navigational and fish-finding aids.

But the heart of this boat, as on any serious fishing machine, is the cockpit. Little Pete has 225 square feet of wide-open fish-fighting space. Along with the usual rod lockers, stowage areas and compartments, it has a splendidly sophisticated fighting chair, a bait-preparation console complete with its own freezer, a fresh-water washdown system for keeping the teakwood deck immaculately clean, two recessed wells with a combined capacity of 48 cubic feet, and a transom door for hauling aboard big fish.

After a hard day's fishing, an angler aboard Little Pete can retire to one of the boat's two double staterooms, each with its own head and dressing area. A 15-by-15-foot saloon sleeps two other people on a convertible sofa. The saloon is also equipped with color television, stereo and a wet bar with an ice machine. And in the galley is a 15-cubic-foot freezer, a full-sized electric stove with an oven, and even a garbage compactor.

The imposing superstructure of the tournament fisherman Little Pete
rises 34 feet above the water as she trolls a stretch of the Atlantic
off the Bahamas. When trolling, the skipper may control the boat from
either the flying bridge, as here, or the tuna tower. The angler, if he
wishes, may remain in air-conditioned comfort below until fish have
been spotted and the crew has made the cockpit ready for action.

Standing on the tuna-tower deck, 34 feet above the water, the skipper steers Little Pete while the mate scans the ocean for fish. A canopy nine feet below holds the rotating radar screen. Beneath it, protected by a solid railing of fiberglass over wood, is the flying bridge.

The view from the tuna tower sweeps away from Little Pete's remarkably clean foredeck to the horizon some seven miles in the distance. On a clear day the total area visible with the naked eye from this excellent vantage point is about 154 square miles.

The control station's focus on the flying bridge is a wheel, beneath which are (1) a tachometer, and engine-pressure and temperature gauges. Combination gear-and-throttle levers for each engine flank the wheel. Under the wheel pedestal (2) are switches for an engine-failure alarm system, windshield wipers, horn and ignition. On the console's port facing (3) are a sea-temperature gauge and clock, while the starboard side (4) contains the automatic pilot and digital depth finder. Under the console top are a radar screen to port (5) and radios to starboard (6). In the bulkhead ahead are a loran (7), recording depth finder (8) and compass (9). Heating rods that operate 24 hours a day control moisture to protect this highly sophisticated equipment.

In the cockpit with a fish on the line, the skipper handles the speed and direction of the boat from the cockpit steering station, while the angler braced in the fighting chair battles the quarry and the mate stands by to assist with a gaff. If the catch turns out to be too large to bring over the side with the gaff, the mate will open the tuna door just to his right and haul the fish aboard through the water-level opening. Little Pete's totally unobstructed railings eliminate any danger of snagging the line, and its nonskid teak deck provides solid footing for the fishermen when the cockpit sole is wet.

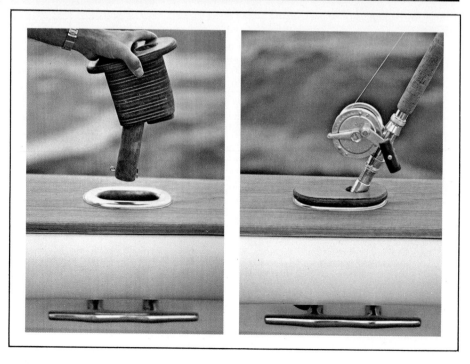

A plug of hardwood surrounding a rod-sized socket drops neatly into a metal hawsepipe —set in the cockpit railing—that serves, at dockside, as a fairlead for mooring lines leading to the cleat below. Out at sea, the socket converts the pipe into a rod holder (far right), allowing extra lines to be trolled.

A bait freezer on the portside bulkhead of the cockpit has a 15-cubic-foot capacity. The frozen bait fish, which have been gutted and prepared for the hook before storing, need about 30 minutes' thawing before use.

Applying the defrosted bait fish to a hook, the mate uses a cutting board placed on a convenient sink-equipped countertop located just above the bait freezer. The towel under the cutting board prevents it from marring the boat's elegantly finished brightwork.

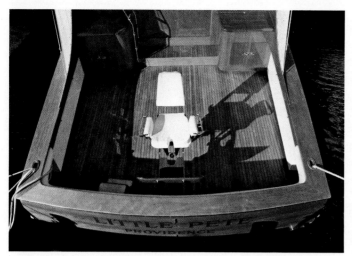

Secured for action, Little Pete's cockpit is a game fisherman's perfect vision of uncluttered efficiency, with nothing in the room-sized after section but the fighting chair. Moreover, every other piece of equipment that a deep-sea fisherman might need lies concealed in lockers (right) within a step or two of the fighting chair.

With its storage areas thrown open, the cockpit reveals an array of
well-designed stowage spaces and neatly arranged gear. Flanking the
fighting chair are a rod locker on the port side (1) and a gaff locker
on the starboard (2). A console (3) for preparing bait has a sink and
freezer. Opposite on the starboard side (4) is a console with steering
controls, a stove and tackle drawers. Flush-mounted in the deck are
two 24-cubic-foot wells (5 and 6) that double as fish boxes or gear
lockers. A third hatch (7) offers access to the boat's generator, and
abaft of the fighting chair (8) is the lazarette where the boarding steps
are stowed. Canvas straps hold open the tuna door in the transom.

2 "You know," said one veteran Gulf Coast angler recently, "most guys don't realize that the captain's the one who really catches the fish." Most novices may not. But every long-time fishing addict like this man is gratefully aware that without an adept boat handler at the helm he would be spending just as productive a day, and a far safer one, if he stayed home and dropped his line in the bathtub. A good fishing-boat skipper operates and maintains his craft so that it consistently performs three vital functions. The first is getting to the fishing grounds in the quickest and most efficient manner. In some cases this may include such mundane chores as cartopping and trailering to a conve-

BOAT HANDLING FOR FISHERMEN

nient launching site near a likely spot, or even mastering the techniques of launching a craft through the surf. Most often, however, it entails the straightforward business of seeing that all gear is stowed safely aboard, checking the weather, and finally plotting the shortest course through the quietest water to the fishing grounds.

Once in the fishing area, the second task begins: actually finding the fish and putting the bait in front of their noses without frightening them off. The art of fish-finding appears to beginners to have almost mystical overtones, but it is actually the result of little more than keen observation of certain relative constants such as wind and current direction, and underwater topography. Recently the art has been abetted by science, in the form of depthfinder and temperature gauges to help pinpoint the precise spot where a given species may be lying on a given day.

With this kind of information in hand, the skipper begins the subtle maneuvering that drops or wiggles the bait into the fish's field of vision. Sometimes this means poking along rocky-bedded rivers; sometimes it means rigging up a kite so as to keep live bait at the water's surface and conceal the line. Most often it means running trolling patterns, the slow but disciplined series of runs and turns that exploit the water methodically and thoroughly. And if other boats are on the trolling grounds, it means adhering to a certain code of courtesy *(pages 68-69)* toward neighboring anglers.

While the general practice in trolling is to keep engine noise and other fish-disturbing sounds to a minimum, the most knowledgeable skippers are aware of certain fascinating exceptions. One is the case of an engine-driven craft passing over a school of striped bass in the open ocean. Though the sound initially scatters the school, which is bad for the fishing, for some reason it also stimulates the urge to feed. To get a bonanza of strikes, therefore, the skipper need only know the right distance behind the boat to troll the lure—not too close to the noisy engine, nor so far back that the urge to feed is gone by the time the bait passes the fish. The best spot is usually the point at which the school begins to re-form in the boat's wake.

Once any fish is hooked, particularly a sizable one, the skipper fulfills his third key function by transforming the boat into an extension of the fisherman's arms and tackle so as to aid in the actual catch. Through his efforts at the helm he actually helps play the fish by moving the boat forward or backward, or by setting it at the best angle for bringing the quarry close aboard. So important is the captain's craft at this point that even the most skilled of fishermen never takes upon himself more than half the credit for landing a fish, saving the balance for the captain. And if the fish is big and the angler relatively new to the game, the captain's balance is even heavier. "With an experienced captain and an inexperienced angler," says one lifetime fisherman who makes boats for a living, "in the case of a giant tuna, for instance, the captain can take 80 per cent of the difficulty out of the fight."

The smooth whirring of an outboard-powered dinghy's propeller barely ripples the surface of a fjord in British Columbia as two men troll for coho salmon on a gray summer morning.

River Fishing

To be consistently successful in fishing a river from a boat, a fisherman must be able to maneuver his craft into the places where fish like to gather, without alarming his skittish prey—or banging his boat into obstacles in midstream or along the banks. As the drawings at right suggest, achieving these objectives in an environment as complex as a river is sure to test a boatman's skills. Besides the currents, shown here with blue arrows, rivers abound with natural hazards—rocks jutting from the river bed, eddies and sudden drops that produce riffles at the least, and sometimes substantial rapids. And these hazards create the very conditions that attract fish—plentiful supplies of both food and oxygen, and breaks in the currents that allow fish to hold easily while they are feeding or resting.

To cope with all these factors, most fishermen find it advisable to work in pairs, one person fishing while the other one is maneuvering the boat—which is described on pages 44-47, where the best boat-handling maneuver for each major section of the river is explained.

Any of these operations must be executed with a minimum of man-made commotion that might distract the fish. When noise—such as an engine or a clanking anchor—is unavoidable, the fisherman should wait at least a few minutes before dipping his line.

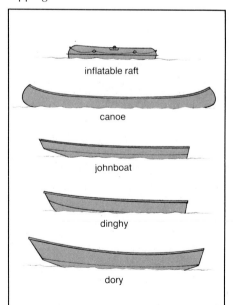

These light, quick-handling, shallow-draft craft can be trailered or car-topped and are easily portaged—all characteristics that suit them to river use. For long runs upstream to the fishing grounds, they can be fitted with an outboard motor, which should be equipped with a grounding shoe to protect the propeller from underwater obstructions.

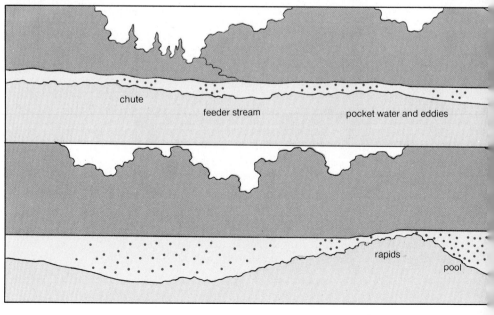

pocket water and eddies

riffles

bend

falls

rapids

pool

The areas of a river that attract fish, shown in dotted patterns in the drawing above, are usually the most difficult stretches to navigate. In the fast-moving current of the chute at upper left, the boatman must apply braking techniques to slow the boat enough for good fishing. At the junction with a feeder stream, he must avoid running aground in shallows. The boulders that create backwaters where fish like to rest can also rip a hull open, and the riffles are miniature rapids. The current at the bend, sluggish on the inside and swift at the outer bank, creates steering problems, and the falls may require a portage.

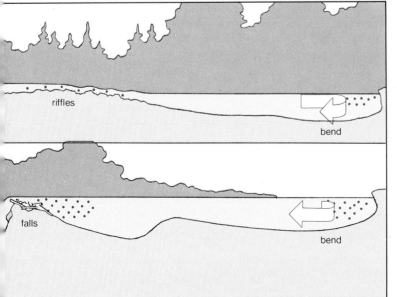

riffles

bend

falls

bend

This two-part cross section reveals the river's piloting hazards, and shows more fully where food settles and fish hold. In the fast-water channel, food is found only near the banks. Food and fish also collect in the slow water at the feeder stream's mouth. Water coursing around boulders forms eddies downstream; between the rock and the eddy is a pocket where fish rest and food drops. The riffle beyond aerates the water, drawing fish to the increased oxygen supply. At the bend, the river undercuts a shady niche on the outer bank where fish hold. And food collects above the lip of the falls and in the pools below.

CHUTE

The current in a chute may carry a free-drifting boat downstream too fast to let a fisherman probe possible fishing holes along the bank. But an oarsman can brake the boat's drift by rowing upstream (1) while his companion, sitting in the stern with an unobstructed view of the water, casts along the shore. Alternatively, the boat can be anchored in midstream (2) in order to give the oarsman a rest, or to allow both men to cast their lines along the river's edge.

Special Anchors and Brakes

Four devices for securing or braking a river fishing boat are shown below. A specialized iron grapnel seizes hard and rocky bottoms; its soft tines bend free when the rode is hauled. A heavy chain acts as a brake when payed out behind a boat. A brush anchor works like ice tongs and can be clipped onto trees or bushes, with a line lashed around its handles. A burlap or heavy plastic bag is an adequate anchor when filled with rocks.

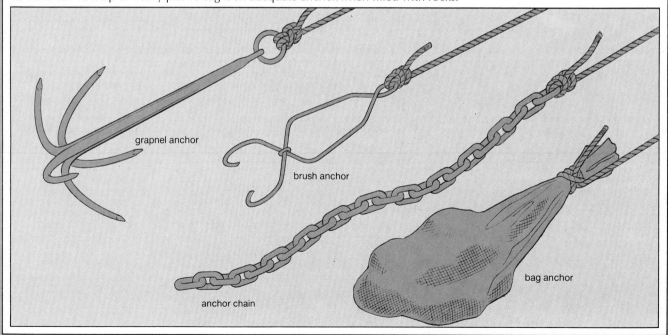

grapnel anchor

brush anchor

anchor chain

bag anchor

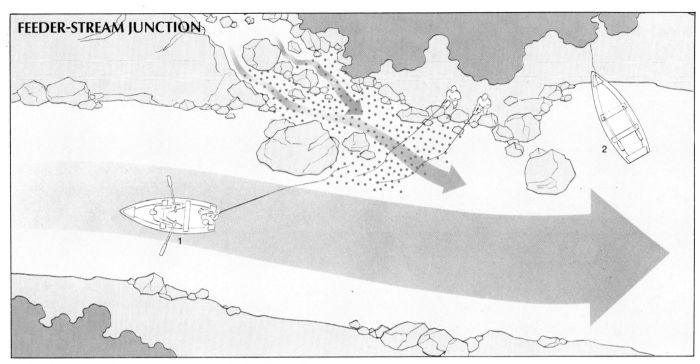

FEEDER-STREAM JUNCTION

Farther downstream, the oarsman may repeat the delaying tactic
of rowing against the current (1) so that the fisherman can cast into
the fish-rich shallows, where a feeder stream adds its nutrients to
those of the river. Alternately the boat can be snubbed to a tree on
the riverbank (2) to allow both anglers to cast their lines from shore.

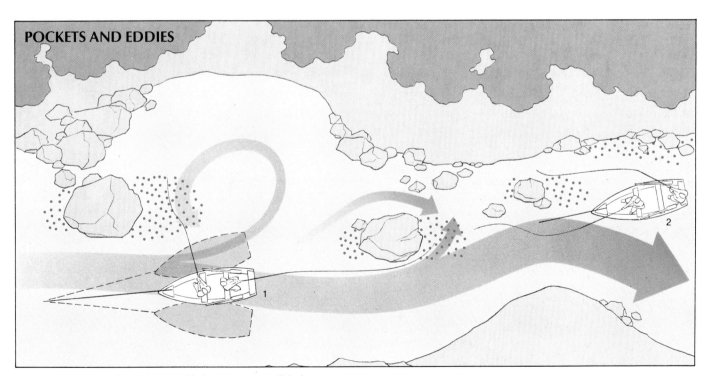

POCKETS AND EDDIES

From a boat anchored in midstream, both crewmen can fish the
pockets created by boulders in the river's current (1). To move the
boat right or left for better access to particular areas, the oarsman
simply thrusts an oar into the water from the appropriate oarlock and
holds the oar firmly in place. The push of the current on the starboard
oar, for example, swings the stern of the boat to port and vice versa
(dotted outlines). The boat can also be anchored (2) 30 feet or more
downstream from the rocks and eddies, out of sight of the fish
that hold in these areas, but close enough for accurate casting upriver.

RIFFLES

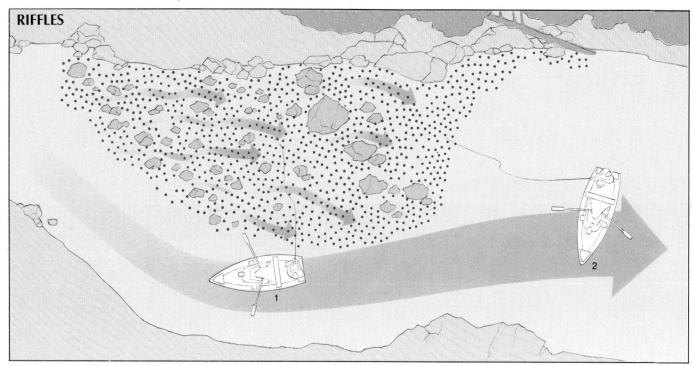

Sliding into a series of riffles, the oarsman guides the boat stern first
along the main channel (above), holding against the current to slow
his speed, while the fisherman casts into the rock-strewn stream
(1). As the boat drifts past the riffles, the oarsman pulls hard with his
starboard oar, swinging the boat broadside to the current (2) to allow
the fisherman a parting cast. Experienced anglers work riffles around
midday, since fish bite in areas of disturbed water then—whereas
in deeper waters they rise to the surface in the morning and evening.

WATERFALLS AND POOLS

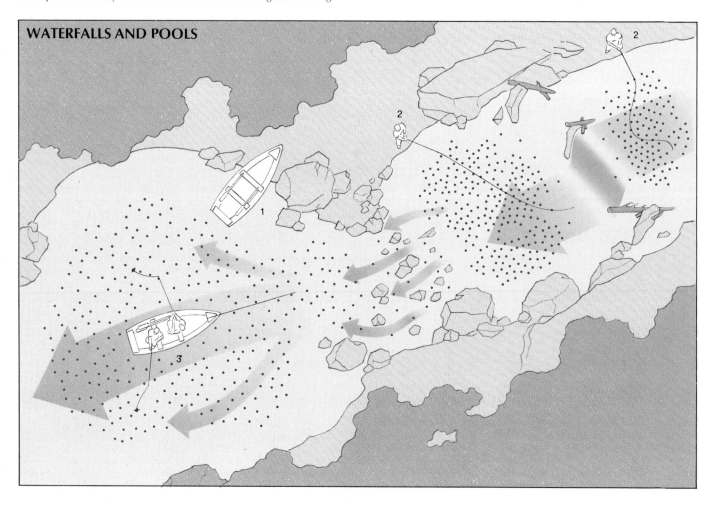

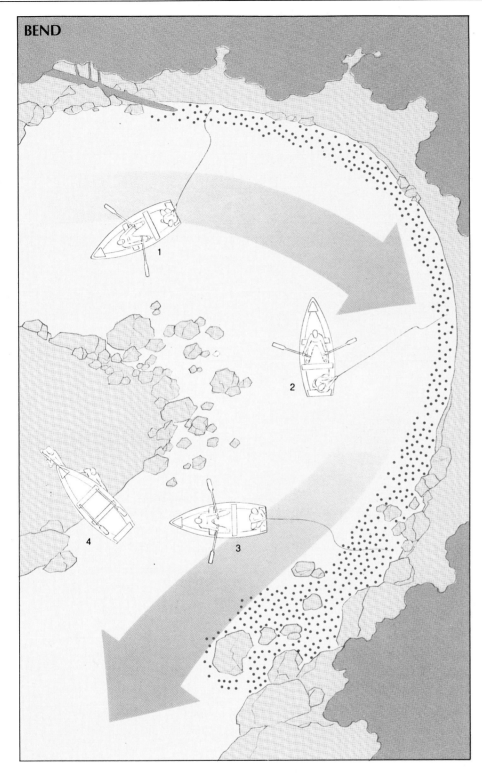

BEND

As the boat approaches a bend, the oarsman again turns his craft stern foremost with a pull on his port oar (1) and steers it into the slower current along the inside of the curve. At this point the fisherman casts along the far bank (2), where the trees and the undercut bank make an attractive holding place for fish by providing shaded protection. As the fisherman plies the far side of the stream, the oarsman steers the boat toward shore on the inside of the curve (3) to avoid the small waterfall ahead. After beaching the boat (4), both angler and oarsman prepare to portage it around the falls (opposite, below).

After completing the portage (opposite at bottom), the boat is left firmly grounded on the riverbank (1). Oarsman and angler backtrack on foot to fish the pools above and just below the falls (2). The falls create a barrier to many upstream fish, which are unable to swim over them, and remain to feed on nutrients collecting in the upper pool. Below the falls, aeration from the tumbling water and food accumulations attract fish from downstream. The first pool below the falls can be fished afoot; the larger one downstream demands that the boat be launched and anchored to still-fish in midstream (3).

Lake Fishing

Before launching a boat to fish a lake of any size, the skipper should devise a plan that takes into account the location of the best probable fishing grounds, the range of the craft, the habits of the prey and the day's weather.

The areas to be fished—which are dotted on the drawing of the prototypal lake at right—can be selected after studying the shoreline and by plotting the underwater topography by means of a contour map *(far right at top)*.

The make-up of these fishing grounds can lead the boatman into some potentially troublesome situations. Seeking out shade and shelter, for example, most lake fish prefer to be near rocky ledges, fallen trees or stands of lily pads. In such spots, the skipper needs all his boat-handling skill to maneuver his vessel close enough to fish without striking the hull on the rocks or entangling the propeller in plant stems. Also, since fish feed most heartily before dawn and at dusk, the trip to the fishing holes is often made in darkness, when boat speeds should be moderate; a powerful spotlight should be aboard to help show the way.

The skipper must also know the weather forecast for the day, then keep an eye peeled for any shift in winds or sudden build-up of storm clouds. When in doubt about fishing or heading in, the skipper should always return to shore.

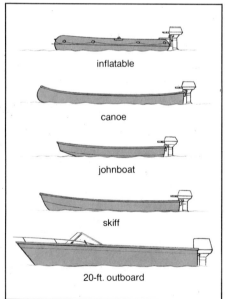

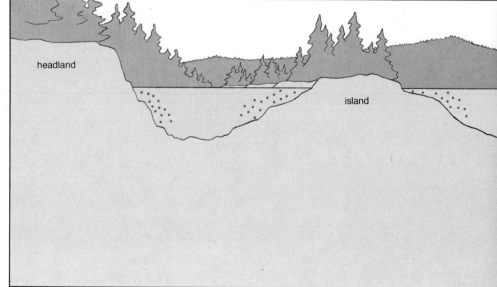

Of these five lake boats the four topmost are light, easily transportable, shallow-draft craft ideal for fishing small- to medium-sized lakes. Less than 20 feet long, they can carry 4- to 10-horsepower outboard motors. The fifth boat, a seaworthy 20-foot outboard, takes a 50- to 100-horsepower motor and can survive all but the worst kinds of weather.

dam

fallen trees

lily pads

A Tip from Topography

A contour map of part of Lake Powell, Utah, shows its underwater topography. Since the lake's normal water level is 3700 feet above the sea, the 3600 contour line is 100 feet deep. The bunched lines in the water mean a steep drop —possibly rock ledges and good fishing.

The prime fishing areas (dots) of this typical lake can be identified through clues in the lakeside terrain. The rocky rise at the woods' edge, with islands opposite, suggests a deep trench with rock outcroppings where fish tend to hide and feed. The dam spills aerated water that draws fish, while stands of lily pads, marsh grasses, and fallen leaves and branches provide feeding grounds and underwater hiding places. Even the wind direction (arrow) is a sign of probable fish location: succulent bugs blown off the land drop onto the water by the windward shore.

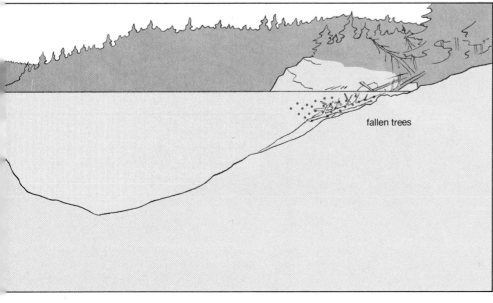

fallen trees

This cross section of the lake above emphasizes the role of underwater terrain in providing fish with cover—and boatmen with potential trouble. The areas where water meets land usually contain plant food and have rocky niches—good haunts for fish, but places to be negotiated carefully by the boatman. Similarly, a downed tree's trunk and branches provide a maze of hideouts for fish, but a source of snares for the boat. In the main lake, the offshore slope contains fish among its rocks and snags; but the drop into deep water, though it provides safe piloting, is an unlikely fishing ground.

Tools for Finding Fish

Since the primary task of any fishing captain is to bring the angler to the fish, many skippers equip their craft with the key fish-finding devices shown here. The simplest of these is a thermometer-depth gauge *(opposite at top right)*, which records the water temperature at specific depths. Because each individual species of game fish prefers its own particular water temperature, the thermometer provides the fisherman with a valuable clue as to how deep to set his lures.

On any lake, temperatures throughout most of the year tend to decrease gradually from surface to lake bottom. But during the prime fishing days of summer the sun heats up the lake's surface, causing a dramatic break in the temperature gradient. The break occurs along an underwater threshold called the thermocline *(opposite at top left)*, and it is here that most of the lake's game fish congregate. Using the thermometer, the fisherman can discover the thermocline's depth and adjust his lines accordingly.

The boatman's other major aid to locating fish is the electronic depth finder shown at left—the same instrument commonly used by navigators. With it he can read the profile of a lake bottom, and thus locate the areas that are likeliest to be rich in fish. An experienced skipper can spot the natural refuges where fish tend to lurk—shipwrecks, reefs, ledges and boulders, or the submerged buildings of impounded lakes. And if a fisherman is both lucky and sharp-eyed, he may pick up echoes from the fish themselves.

dial

lake bottom

single fish

school of fish

transducer

school of fish

single fish

lake bottom

An electronic depth finder reads underwater contours through a transducer in the hull's bottom. The transducer sends electronic pulses and receives the echoes that bounce off the bottom—or off the fish. This information appears either as illuminated lines on a dial (top), or as stylus marks on a moving roll of graph paper (bottom). In these drawings, the fine lines between 30 and 45 feet on both the dial and graph signal a school of fish, and the marking at 70 feet indicates a single large fish. The solid band from 75 to 80 feet on the dial is the rocky bottom, which shows as a continuous profile on the graph.

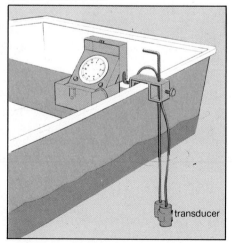

transducer

A portable depth finder, which can be mounted on a small outboard, works the same as the more sophisticated instrument explained at left; but it is far simpler to install —and is about five times cheaper. The portable transducer is simply hung overboard from an aluminum pipe clamped to the boat. The dial housing is placed on any convenient seat, or set in a bracket on the gunwale.

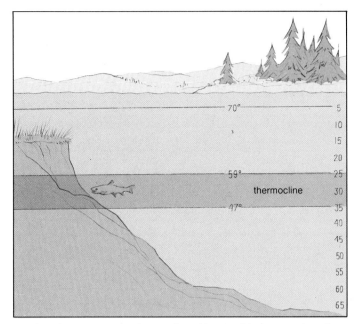

A coho salmon swims the thermocline (blue) in this cross section of a lake in summer. An area of abrupt temperature transition between the warm upper water and the cold lower levels, the thermocline occurs at different depths in every lake. Here, it encompasses the sector where the temperature falls from 59° to 47°, a drop of 12° in just 10 feet. By contrast, in the warm layers above the thermocline, the temperature drop is only 11° in a full 20 feet of water.

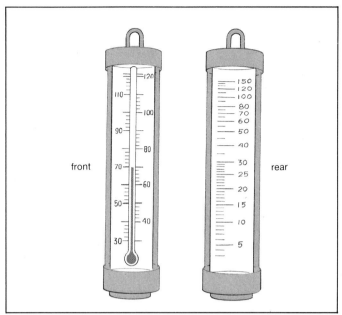

A combination thermometer and depth gauge, shown here from front and back, allows a fisherman to determine the vertical locus of the thermocline. To get a reading, the instrument is lowered overboard to any depth and held for 20 seconds while water enters a one-way valve, and the temperature and depth are recorded. The fisherman then retrieves the instrument and notes the readings. After several soundings, he can judge the boundaries of the thermocline.

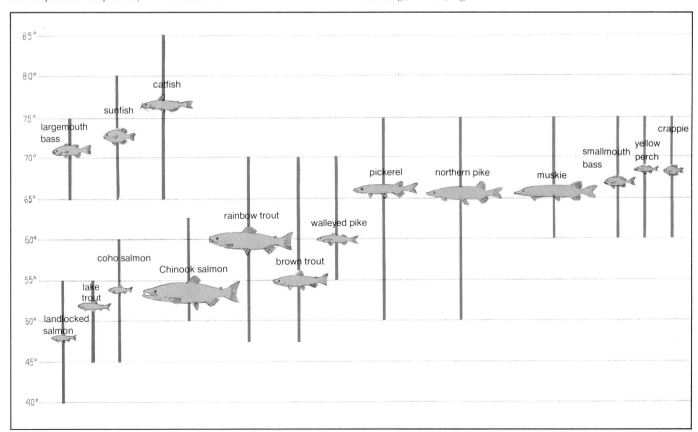

The preferred temperature ranges for some of the most common U.S. fresh-water game fish vary from near tropical to frigid. The catfish usually swims near the surface of the warmest lakes, where the water has a bathtub temperature of 75° and more. The largemouth bass and sunfish also have a high tolerance for warm water. But most of the other popular game fish—including pickerel, pike, and some trout and salmon—live in relatively cool water that ranges from 65° to 55°. The landlocked salmon seeks the lowest depths of the coolest lakes where the water temperature is a wintry 45°.

One common practice when trolling a lake is to deploy four lines, two from the sides of the boat and two from stern positions, as indicated in the top picture below. During exploration, these lines are trolled at carefully calculated lengths and depths (middle picture, below). Because fish resting near the bottom may be attracted by the motor's vibration, the shorter lines—whose lures can benefit most from this stimulation—are weighted to run deep, one just off the bottom and one at midwater. Of the longer lines, one is fished on the surface; the other, lightly weighted, is trolled three to four feet deep.

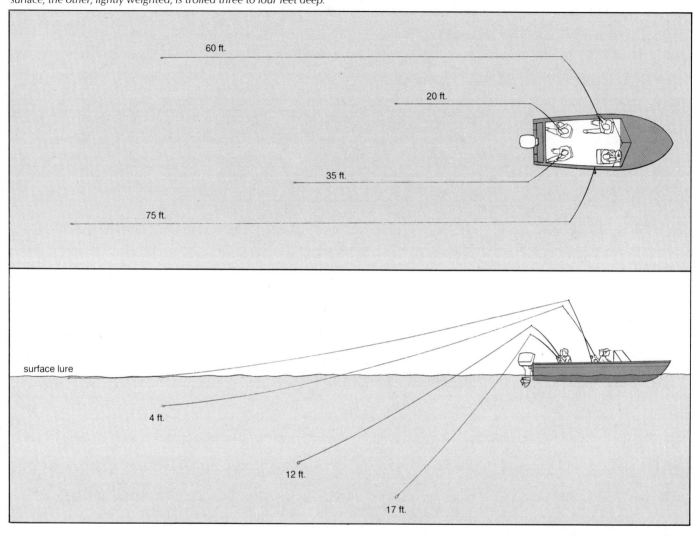

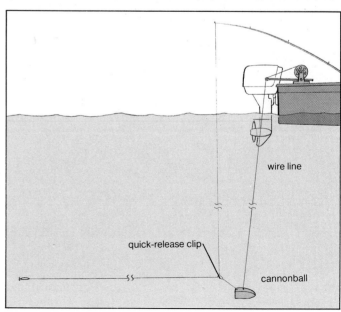

The downrigger mounted on the boat at right is the most effective of the many devices designed to hold a trolled lure at a precise depth. The downrigger consists of a reel, 100 feet or more of wire line, an 8- to 10-pound weight (popularly known as a cannonball), and a quick-release clip attached just above the weight. The fisherman snaps the clip around his baited line and then lowers the weight and attached line to the chosen depth. When a fish strikes, the line pulls free, permitting the fisherman to play his catch unhindered.

Fresh-Water Trolling

Ever since the advent of the outboard motor in the early 1900s, trolling—trailing a lure or bait behind a moving boat—has been a favorite technique of the sport fisherman. The advantage of trolling over casting is that the fisherman is able to search more water in less time, while trying out several different rigs and lures simultaneously.

When two or more fishermen set out to troll, the more experienced hand generally takes the helm first, during the exploratory phase, in which the fish are located by means of several systematic trolling patterns *(overleaf)*. Lines are deployed so as to sweep the water at a variety of depths, as shown opposite. Several speeds are also tried *(right and below)*.

When the fish begin to strike, the trollers switch to the so-called production phase. They adjust all the trolling lines to roughly the same length and depth as the successful line, and continue to make passes over the area. Keeping a steady speed when trolling in the wind and when executing turns—maneuvers that tend to slow the boat and sink the lures—now becomes a critical factor, calling for use of the boat-handling techniques shown on pages 56-57.

A fisherman whose boat lacks a speedometer can gauge his trolling speed accurately with the homemade device below—modeled on a venerable navigational tool called a chip log. Cut a six-inch length of broomstick and tie one end of a 140-foot length of strong, nonstretch fishing line securely around the stick's waist, as shown. Then, at 22-foot intervals in the line, tie overhand knots. Coil the line to run freely. Toss the chip log in the water and let the line run through the fingers for exactly 15 seconds. The number of knots that have slipped out is equal to the boat's speed in statute miles per hour.

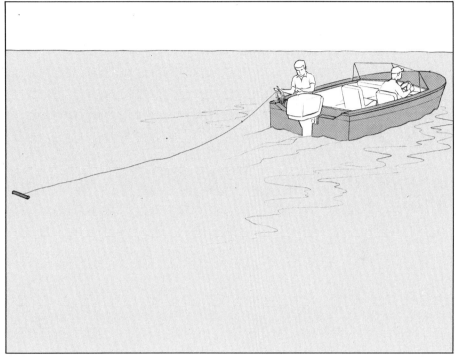

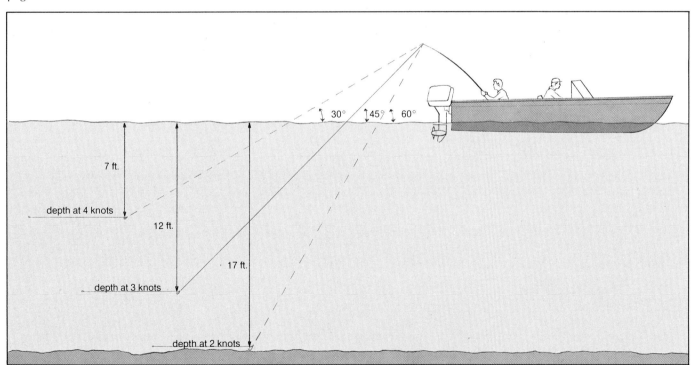

Once the angler finds his optimum speed, he can frequently maintain it by watching the angle at which his line enters the water, and adjusting his speed to keep that angle constant. This procedure exploits the fact that an increase in the boat's speed will cause the lure to rise above its previous level. Thus, when the boat above travels at three knots, its lure rides at a depth of 12 feet and the line makes a 45° angle with the water's surface. If he speeds up to four knots, the lure rises to seven feet, and the line enters the water at 30°.

When a trolling boat makes a turn, the boat itself describes a wider arc than the lines trailing behind. Since the lures thus travel a shorter distance than the boat, they have a tendency to slow down and sink in a turn. And, if the boatman is not careful, the lines may tangle each other. To prevent this, whenever possible the boatman should make his turns in the direction of the longer line, which naturally describes the sharpest arc. If he must turn toward the shorter line, the fisherman should reel in that line far enough to hold it clear of the longer one, then pay it out after the turn has been completed.

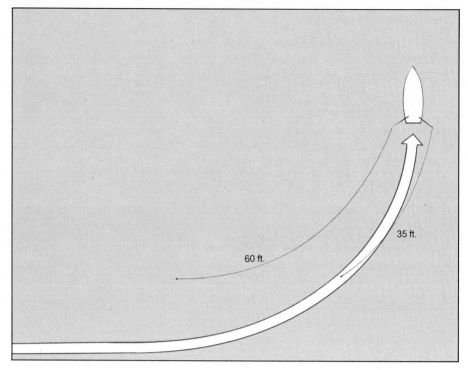

To liven up the motion of a lure moving through the water, the boatman could choose to steer the weaving course shown here. Because the fishing lure is turning less than the boat and thus slowing down, it will sink slightly with each turn, adding vertical as well as horizontal action to its motion.

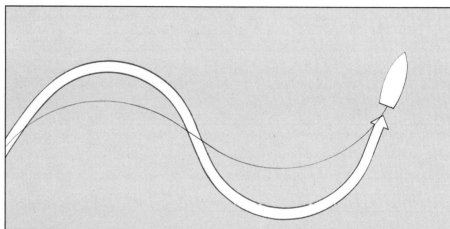

For exploratory trolling along a shoreline, the boatman starts his pattern in deep water and works toward the shallows, systematically moving in on any fish that may be feeding there. Typically he begins at a depth of 20 feet, as shown by the outer bottom contour; then he makes a series of passes, adjusting the trolling lines to the decreasing depths as he goes. At the end of each sweep he turns away from the shore toward the deeper water —thus avoiding any danger of hitting bottom on the turn. He then comes back in for the next sweep. The overlapping figure eights thus described cover the area thoroughly.

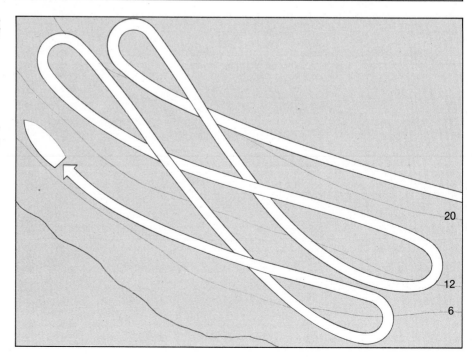

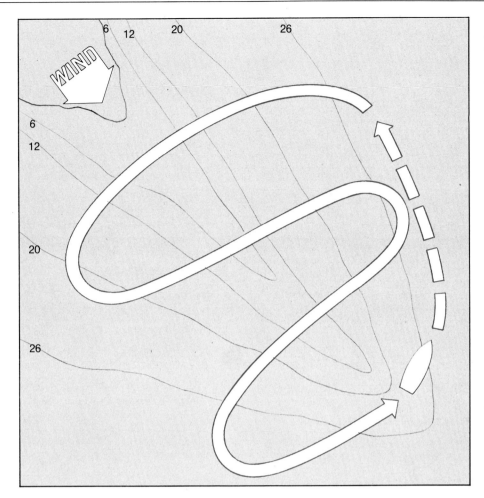

When trolling on a windy day, the boatman should set his pattern at right angles to the breeze so that the wind neither increases nor impedes the boat's speed during each pass. In the example shown, the wind is blowing down a ledge that extends underwater, so the boatman begins upwind and works outward. This allows him to make his turns downwind to gain a momentary extra thrust of speed just when his lures would otherwise slow down and sink. The only time he heads into the wind is when he returns to his starting position to repeat his passes (dashed arrow).

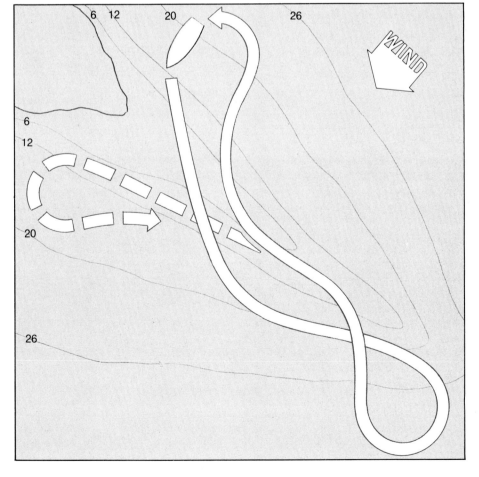

When the wind blows across a ledge, the troller generally makes weaving patterns down the length of the ledge and back in order to keep the wind abeam. In working the shoal area shown here, the boatman can run alternately along one side of the adjacent point of land and then the other (dashed arrow) to extend his trolling area. He must be careful when turning on the windward side to start his downwind turn well offshore.

Handling a Lunker

When a good-sized fish—called a lunker by fresh-water anglers—takes the bait and runs with it, both the fisherman and the boat's helmsman must respond instantly, and with perfect teamwork, to take tension off the fishing tackle and keep the catch from breaking away. The fisherman moves as quickly as possible to an unobstructed position—normally in the bow —to play the fish. At the same time, the boatman begins using his engine almost as though it were an extension of the angler's rod and reel, first giving the fish plenty of scope for the initial run, then acting as a drag to slow the fish down and bring it alongside.

If the boat is at anchor when the fish strikes, the boatman's first order of business is to cast off, as described at right. Then, having switched on his motor, he gives chase. The proper speed during the pursuit will depend upon the behavior and size of the fish. A 40- to 60-pound lake trout or muskie, for example, may take off at speeds up to 10 or 12 miles per hour; the helmsman's response should be to speed up to four miles per hour, fast enough to lighten the load on the angler's line but slow enough to brake and fatigue the fish as it goes. Should the fish make any abrupt turns in midcareer, the boatman quickly follows suit. The only exception to this rule occurs when it becomes necessary to steer a fish away from other boats or shallow-water obstructions, as described at bottom right.

Finally, when the endurance test between man and fish is near its end, the boatman cuts the engine so he can assist in netting and landing the big prize (opposite, bottom).

To facilitate quick pursuit after a fish strikes, a thoughtful boatman keeps the on-board end of his anchor rode tied to a flotation device so that it can be tossed away instantly, as shown, for retrieval later on. While the fisherman sits momentarily to steady the boat, the boatman moves aft to start his motor and turn the boat toward the fish.

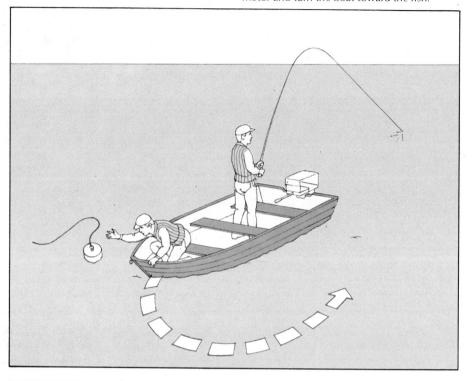

A Timely Move Away from Trouble

The moment some fish, like the muskie and the largemouth bass, feel the hook, they head for cover—shallow water, weeds, lily pads—where the craft cannot safely maneuver. If light tackle prevents the angler from reeling in the still-fighting fish, the job falls to the boatman, who puts the engine in very slow reverse and backs away. The move is, at best, risky, for the extra strain may break the line.

Once the boat is underway, the angler, having moved to the bow where he can play the fish most easily, fine-tunes the tension on his line, while the helmsman slowly moves the boat ahead to ease most of the strain. The throttle is set below the potential speed of the fish, to tire it. The boatman now reels in any extra lines so they will not foul.

Keeping a close watch on the angle of the fisherman's rod and line relative to the bow of the boat, the helmsman can respond quickly to any change in course that the fish might take, and so keep his bow pointed right on target. Thus, if the fish should veer to port, as shown here, the helmsman swings the boat over with the fish.

When the angler thinks his fish is played out, he and the boatman agree which side to take it on. The boatman turns accordingly and throttles down to bring the craft gently alongside the fish. He then cuts the engine and, as a precaution against a final, line-tangling rush by the fish, tilts the motor to bring the propeller out of the water.

As the angler reels in the fish, the boatman gets a net under it, as shown, or hooks it with a gaff (pages 76-77). Whichever method is used, the equipment must be ready and within easy reach; a wasted second at this critical moment could allow the fish to slip away. Once the fish is boated, the helmsman takes the craft back to find the anchor.

Cartopping

The simplest way to haul a lightweight fishing craft is to lash it securely to the top of a car. Almost any boat under 12 feet long is a candidate for cartopping; longer boats usually must be trailered. And just about any car makes a suitable transport vehicle, provided it is equipped either with a metal roof rack, or with a carrier device like the one at right, which helps secure the boat and distribute its weight.

Automobile accessory stores carry a variety of such cartopping devices. The two most popular models are similar in design, with twin metal or wooden bars running across the car's width, each with its own strap for securing the boat. The difference between the two is in the way they are affixed to the roof. On one type, the carrier bars are fitted with suction cups that cling to the roof, and with a strap and metal catch at either end that hooks onto the rain gutter. On the other type *(right)*, a pair of metal brackets, which clamp either into the gutter or into the frame just above the doors, support the carrier bar.

Loading the boat onto the carrier requires both muscle and finesse; but here again the boatman can rig up a helpful accessory. One such device eases the task of one-man loading *(opposite, below)*, while another simplifies the job for either a one- or two-man crew *(right, below)*.

In cartopping, the boat is always loaded onto the car upside down with the bow forward—thus reducing wind resistance—and lashed down bow and stern to prevent the wind from working it loose.

Nylon lines make the best lashings, since their elasticity absorbs vibrations and shocks. But nylon is very slippery when wet; the boatman should check the tension in his lines whenever he stops—or if he feels the boat vibrating. These lines are attached to the front and rear bumpers by one of three methods. Older cars and most heavy-duty vehicles have projecting bumpers on which to tie the lines. On newer-model cars with bumpers flush to the grille, the line can be attached to an S hook that is slipped under the bumper. Or the boatman can drill holes in the front and rear bumpers, and secure eyebolts; the drilled areas must be touched up with chrome paint to prevent rust.

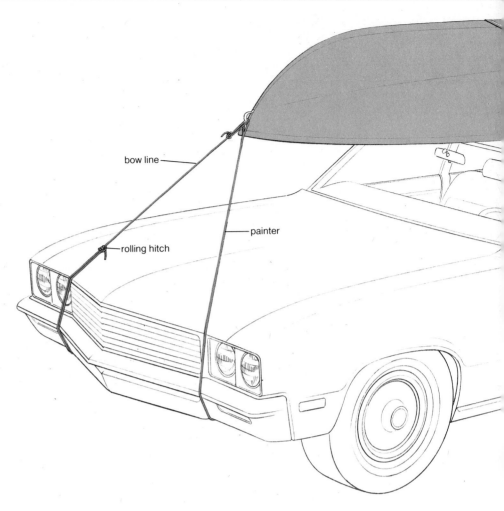

bow line

painter

rolling hitch

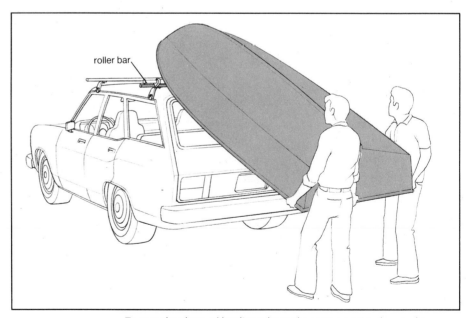

roller bar

To ease the chore of loading a boat, the cartop carrier shown above has been fitted with a roller bar. On a square-back vehicle such as a station wagon, the roller is affixed to the rear carrier bar, and the boat is loaded from the back, as here. If the car is a sedan or coupe with a broad horizontal trunk, the roller must be installed lengthwise between the two carrier bars, and the boat loaded from the side. In that case, the boatman first places the bow of the boat on the roller and pushes the craft up onto the roof. He then turns the boat so that the bow faces forward and the hull nestles securely in place.

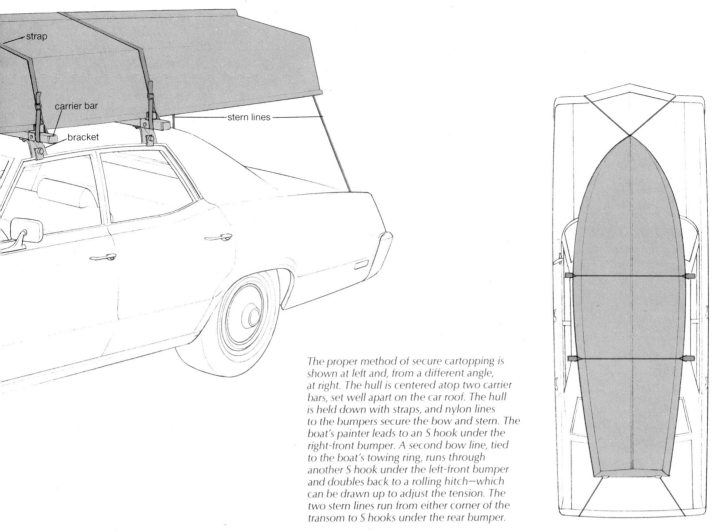

strap

carrier bar

bracket

stern lines

The proper method of secure cartopping is shown at left and, from a different angle, at right. The hull is centered atop two carrier bars, set well apart on the car roof. The hull is held down with straps, and nylon lines to the bumpers secure the bow and stern. The boat's painter leads to an S hook under the right-front bumper. A second bow line, tied to the boat's towing ring, runs through another S hook under the left-front bumper and doubles back to a rolling hitch—which can be drawn up to adjust the tension. The two stern lines run from either corner of the transom to S hooks under the rear bumper.

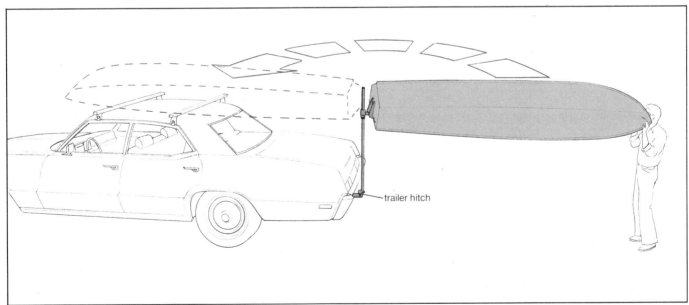

trailer hitch

A solitary boatman can swing his craft from the ground onto a car with the loading rig seen above. The loader has a vertical metal pole that bolts onto the car's trailer hitch through a special adapter. On this pole is a set of screw clamps, which the boatman positions at the level of the car's roof. The boatman turns his craft upside down with the stern facing the trunk, and lifts the stern until the transom can be slipped into the set of clamps, which he tightens. He raises the bow and walks the boat around until it is facing forward (arrow). Finally, the boatman adjusts the craft on the carrier and secures it.

Salt-Water Fishing

The angler who goes down to the sea in a boat enters a far more complex world than that of his fresh-water cousin. Whether he voyages miles beyond sight of land, or ranges a coastline like the one charted at right, he must know how to deal not only with the feeding habits and evasive tactics of scores of game-fish species, but also with the vagaries and hazards of the ocean itself. When fishing a beach, he may need to launch his boat through the surf *(page 62)*. The boatman must take into account swift currents that can sweep his craft off course and tangle trolling lines. He must be aware of tidal ranges that are great enough in some places to totally strand a grounded craft. And he must keep a close eye on wind and weather that can quickly turn a quiet beach into a dangerous lee shore.

In pursuit of this challenging sport, salt-water anglers make use of the same tools that help guide any seaman. They need compasses to find faraway fishing grounds, and to make it home in a fog. Their craft must be outfitted with running lights, which are required by law, and radiotelephones to call for help in the event of an emergency.

Charts are particularly useful to the salt-water fisherman, for the very obstacles that pilots are at great pains to avoid are frequently the favorite haunts of fish. And a fisherman who is armed with a chart not only can pinpoint a potential hot spot, he is also able to troll it without running aground.

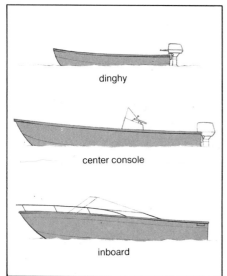

A 12-foot dinghy with a 10-hp outboard motor is one of the best choices for trolling within three miles of shore; a center console with an 80-hp outboard extends the range over 40 miles; an inboard motor and a deeper-draft hull will provide a steady ride in rough water.

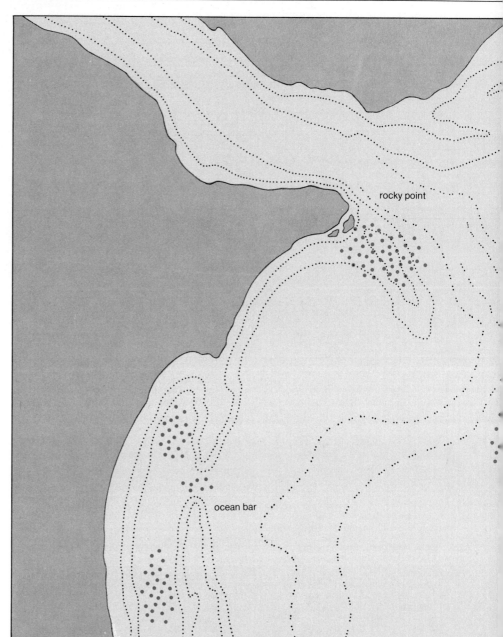

rocky point

ocean bar

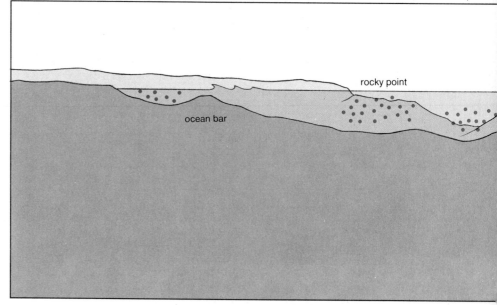

rocky point

ocean bar

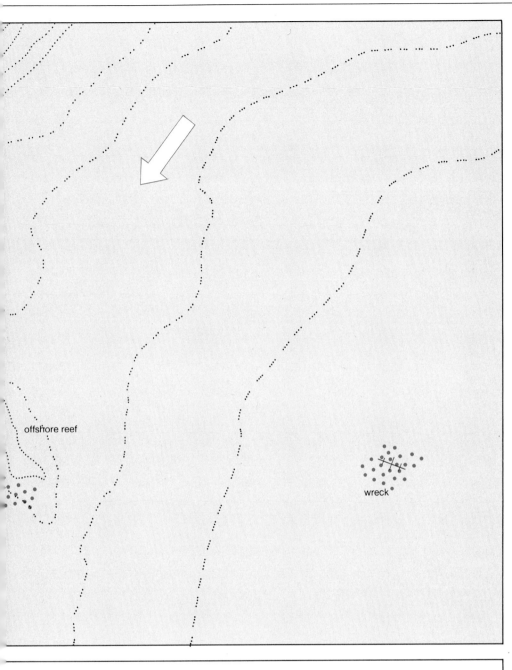

A simulated fishing ground, extrapolated from actual coastal charts, exemplifies the kinds of tricky underwater terrain that provide cover for game fish (represented by dots). For example, the rocky point with a current (blue arrow) sweeping by, the inlet through an ocean bar, the wreck and the offshore reef are all likely spots for a catch. They also suggest specially modified trolling techniques, as shown in the excerpted sections reproduced on pages 64-67.

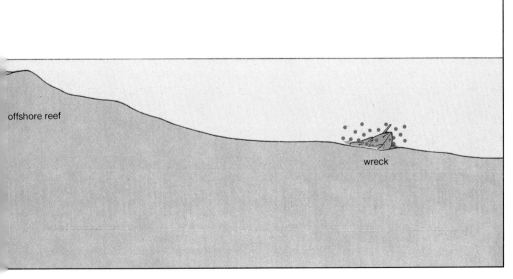

A cross section of the simulated fishing ground charted above shows the elevations of its underwater topography. In trolling such waters, the boatman must coordinate the lengths of his trolling lines and the speed of his boat with the changing depths of the water that surrounds these features, so that his lines will reach deep enough to catch fish without fouling on the bottom.

To launch a skiff from a beach into the surf, two men slide the boat,
bow first and outboard cocked up, into the outrun from a broken
wave (upper left). As the boat begins to float, one man leaps aboard
and begins to row while the other shoves from astern (upper right) to
get it past the next incoming breaker. When the boat is afloat, the
second man jumps aboard (lower left), then lowers the outboard and
starts the motor (lower right) while the oarsman ships his oars.

To land a boat through the surf, a motorman runs the engine while
riding the crest of a wave and heading toward shore (left).
His passenger keeps his weight amidships so that the bow will run
smoothly up onto the sand. When the boat grounds out (right),
the motorman lifts the outboard motor, as his companion makes
ready to leap out onto the beach holding the boat's painter to haul
the boat ashore, securely beyond reach of the next breaker.

A Pole for Sand Flats

Along the sand flats of Florida and the Bahamas, boatmen stalk the skittish bonefish in shallow-draft boats that they guide by poling—thus eliminating the disturbing put-put of an engine. In very shoal water, with the outboard raised, the poler stands erect to see ahead and to get a good purchase on the pole (upper drawing). To propel the boat, he jams the tip of the pole against the bottom and shoves it aft in a rhythmic, hand-over-hand motion (pages 98-99). His pole is as much as 18 feet long, with a rounded fork at the lower end to prevent the tip from sinking into the sand, and a sharp mooring spike at the upper end. His passenger sits low in the boat, watching with binoculars for bonefish tails breaking the surface, a telltale sign that occurs when the fish upend themselves to feed off the bottom. When the boatmen have sighted a school, the poler reverses the pole, pushes the spearlike tip into the sand, grips it firmly with both hands and sits down to give the fisherman room to cast.

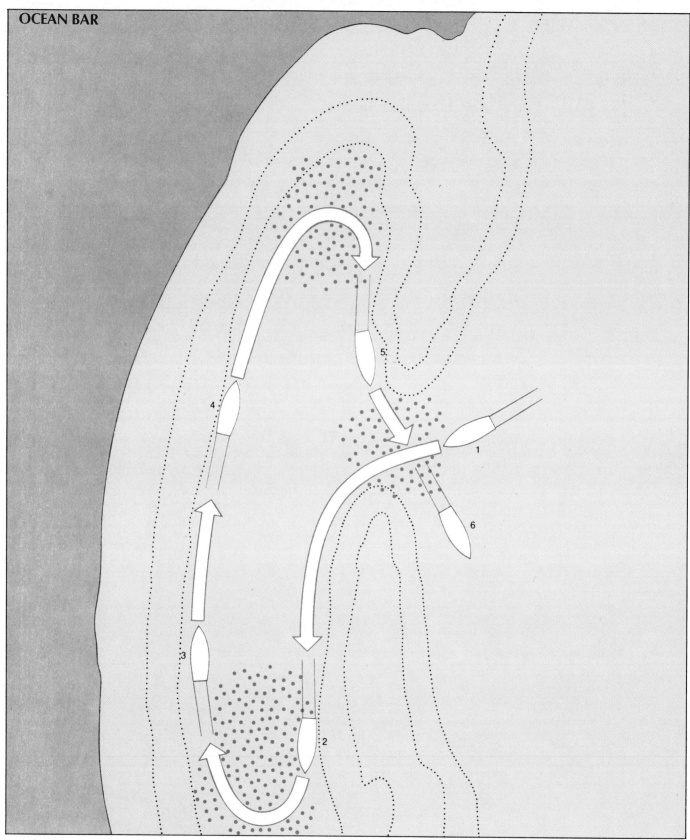

OCEAN BAR

To troll a shore front guarded by sunken sandbanks, the fisherman finds an inlet with a navigable entrance, as in this excerpt from the map on pages 60-61. He runs in at three to four knots while letting out line (1). When the water gets too shallow and he must turn (2), he accelerates to five knots to lift his lines off the bottom, then slows to about two knots (3), a minimum trolling speed. If no fish strikes, he trolls along the beach at three to four knots (4) to pick up any strays. After cruising over any particularly likely spot, he slows again (5) to minimum speed. On leaving the inlet (6), he pulls in and checks lines.

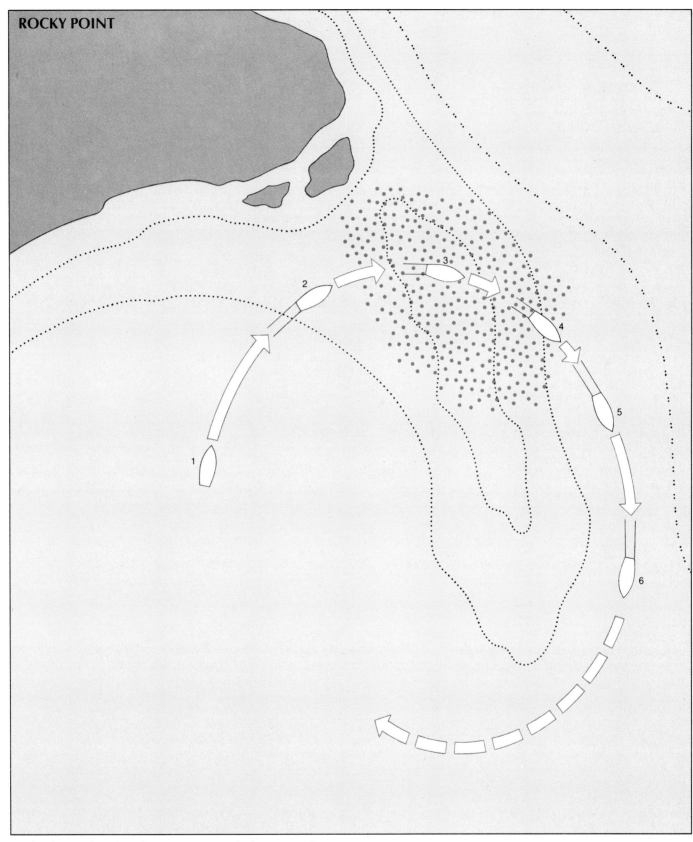

ROCKY POINT

Heading for a rocky point, where snags are a particular menace, the troller baits and begins to set lines as he approaches (1). He cuts to a trolling speed of four knots as the depth finder indicates shoaling water (2), and then, in the shallowest water (3), he shortens lines to 50 or 60 feet to pull them off the bottom. On leaving the shoal waters (4), he slows to about three knots to sink the lures. As the water deepens (5), he throttles back to two knots or less and lengthens lines to over 100 feet so that the lures will sweep down the incline of the reef. Once past the reef (6), he pulls in lines and circles again.

When a boatman sights a surface-swimming school of game fish, which can range in size from two-pound stripers to large tuna, as indicated here, he slows from his cruising speed, sets his trolling lines and runs on a course that brings him about 10 yards in front of the school. As he comes in line with the course of the school, he turns directly away from it (dashed line) and carefully adjusts his speed so that the fish gradually overtake the baits, which are set on lines of equal length to give the illusion of a school of fish.

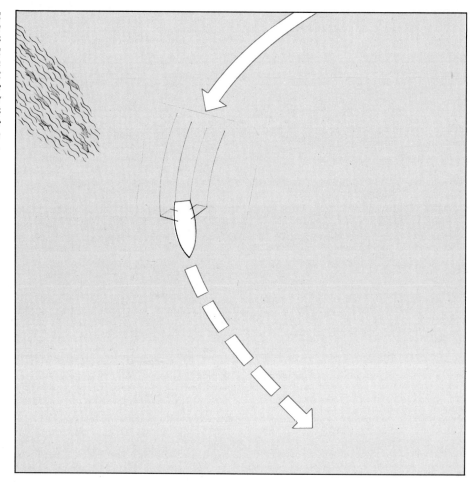

If a boatman spots a single large fish, like a marlin or swordfish, he starts his interception just as he would for a school (above). To swing both baits in front of the fish and increase the chance that the fish will take one, the skipper swerves in regular curving patterns (dashed arrow), pulling the baits slightly broadside to the fish on each turn.

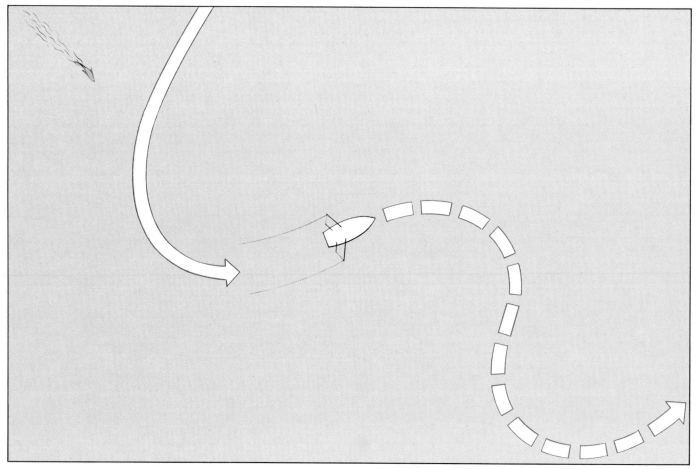

To troll for voracious eaters like bluefish or mackerel, which tend to ball up near the surface when feeding, a boatman tries to drag his lures through the circle of fish without driving his boat across them. He sets his baits 100 or more feet astern, cuts in close to the circle and then steers around it (solid line). The lines will lag slightly through the turn. As a result, the lures are pulled through the feeding fish, even though the boat has only skirted the school. The boatman then heads straight away from the circle (dashed arrow) to check his lines and rebait, if necessary, before repeating the maneuver.

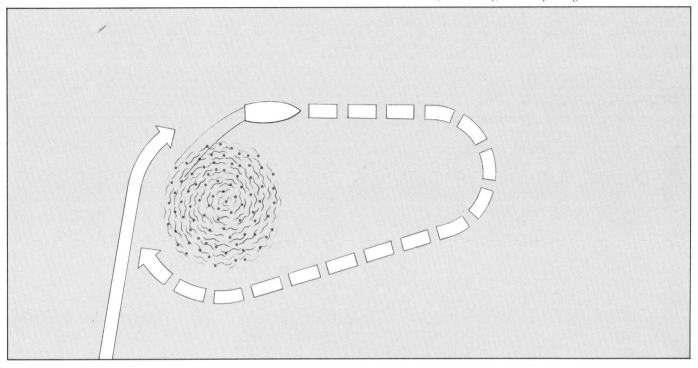

How to Troll a Rip

Game fish often congregate in a kind of turbulent water known as a rip, where swift current flowing over a reef or other large projection from the bottom causes smaller fish to tumble, making them easy prey. To troll such water, the boatman approaches from up-current so as not to spook the fish. Then, holding his bow at 45° to the flow, he enters in front of the rip from one side, allowing his lures to trail back into the turbulent area. Once his lines are into the rip, he carefully modulates the boat speed so as not to move ahead or slip back, while the current acting on his angled bow sweeps his craft sideways.

Observing Etiquette

Salt-water trolling is seldom a solitary sport. Fishing boats and anglers regularly congregate at a favorite spot during ebb or flood tidal runs, when schools of such fish as striped bass, bluefish and mackerel rise from the bottom to seek food. If the fish are indeed biting, dozens of boats may swarm over the same area and indulge in a pastime that oldtimers call "fishing from each other's hip pockets."

To maneuver a boat at proper trolling speed through such crowded waters requires a combination of both skillful boat handling and an unusual degree of cooperation by all skippers in the vicinity. Over the years, certain rules of trolling etiquette have evolved to help maintain order. And though these rules may vary slightly from place to place, if a skipper follows the ones set forth on these pages, he will generally be able to avoid crossing boats, lines or tempers on any fishing ground in the United States.

Dos and Don'ts for Trollers

- Never troll in an area already being fished by casting boats. If the area is spacious enough to accommodate both types of fishing, the trolling boats customarily work well offshore of the casting boats, which prefer to fish among the inshore rocks with surface plugs.

- Since boats traveling at high speed often spook fish for a considerable distance, make your approach to a trolling area as slowly as possible—at no more than five knots—to avoid disturbing the fish. Leave slowly, too, accelerating gradually as distance increases; full throttle should be avoided anywhere within one quarter mile of a fishing ground.

- Don't use trolling techniques so different from those of the other boats in the area that they create confusion for both fish and fishermen. For example, don't surface troll where others are deep trolling. And never set a course that runs counter to the established pattern of trolling traffic.

- Don't pull alongside a trolling boat and expect its crew to provide on-the-spot information on how and what the fish are biting. You're supposed to figure that out for yourself. It's also considered poor form to ask for such information by radio, although you are free to glean whatever tidbits you can by listening in on radio conversations between nearby boats. If you still want information, wait until a successful boat has stopped fishing and is heading home before approaching the skipper.

- When entering a trolling pattern, avoid the temptation to fall in close behind a successful boat. The other skipper may decide to take you on a wild-fish chase by deliberately heading into a fishless area in order to get rid of you.

- In crowded areas, where space between boats is tight, avoid excessively long lines and maintain a uniform trolling speed.

- When running free, always give trolling boats the courtesy of a wide berth.

- In heavy traffic, establish a predictable trolling course and stick with it.

- Never anchor in a trolling area. If you decide to take a fishing break, look for a spot unlikely to attract trolling boats.

- Don't swim in trolling areas. Swimming not only scares fish but creates a hard-to-see hazard for trolling fishermen. Skin divers display a red warning flag with a diagonal white stripe when diving in any boating area.

- Avoid unnecessary noise afloat, like loud music and needless shouting. It carries far downwind, interferes with necessary communication and generally irritates other fishermen.

- Don't pollute a trolling area by dumping. If you want to mark a patch of water where the fish seem especially active, use soluble vegetable oil—which creates a temporary slick. Insoluble gasoline or lubricating oil should never be used.

- Never turn so abruptly in front of another boat that it has to reverse engines or swerve sharply to avoid a collision—even if you have the right of way.

- Never turn so close behind another boat as to pass over and possibly cut its lines.

- If you do accidentally cut another boat's lines, you are expected to stop, apologize and offer replacement tackle from your on-board supply.

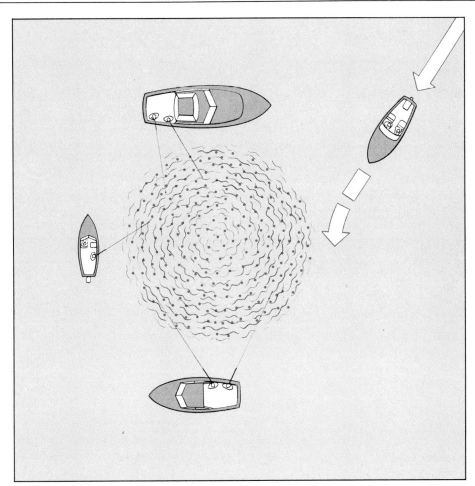

When entering a circle of boats like this one, in which fishermen are casting into a closely bunched school of feeding fish, the skipper of the newly arrived boat (near left) first circles beyond the perimeter. The other boats are expected to adjust their positions, as the three here have done, to give the newcomer an equal portion of the perimeter. The fourth boat then noses into its allotted space.

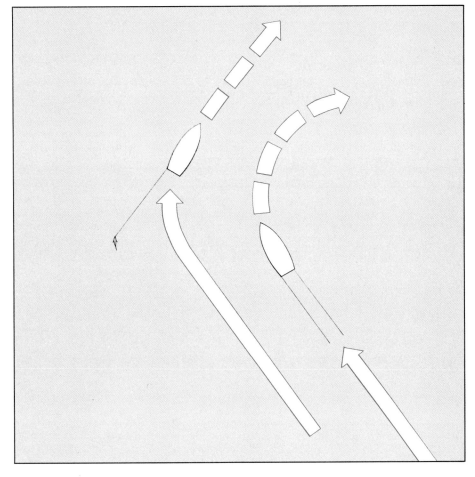

A boat with a hooked fish, like the one at far left, traditionally claims the right of way over a boat that is trolling free. Here, the successful boat has slowed and is heading out of its trolling pattern while its catch is being reeled in. The following boat prepares to make a tight turn to starboard to open the distance between them. If the hooked fish is a big fighter like a tuna, which may take as much as 30 minutes or more to land, the engaged skipper may hoist a red flag to warn other boats to keep their distance.

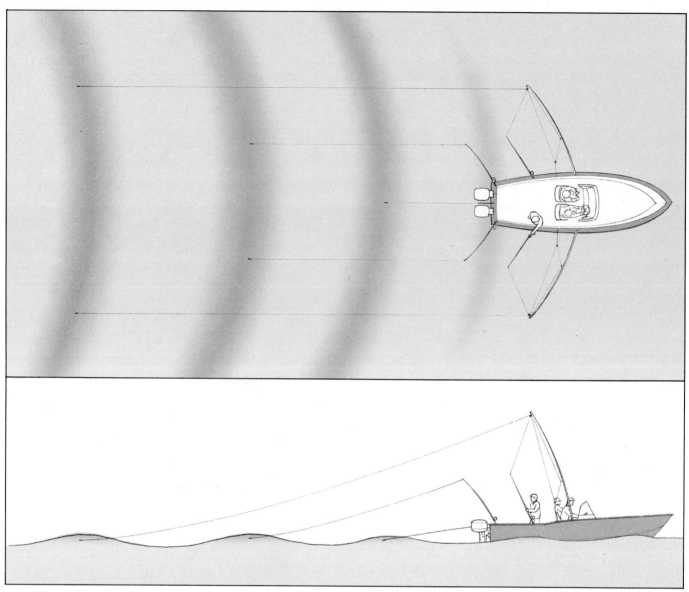

A five-line trolling rig, commonly used in offshore tuna fishing, is set out with line lengths adjusted so the lures ride the crests of three successive stern waves (the bow wave is omitted from the drawing). As in most big game fishing, the boat travels at four to seven knots. The longest lines are held by the ends of outriggers on either side of the boat. The middle lines are attached to rods fitted into holders at the stern. The short line pulls a hookless teaser, or an oversized lure, to tempt the curious tuna.

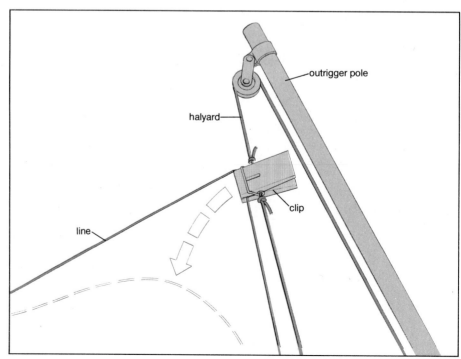

This view of an outrigger tip reveals the standard method for rigging a deep-sea trolling line. With the rod secured in a holder near the base of the outrigger pole, the line is run through a spring clip, which is hoisted to the tip of the outrigger pole by a halyard. When a fish strikes the lure, the shock pulls the line free from the clip (arrow) and drops it into the water. This creates a momentary slack in the line, allowing the fish to take the bait undisturbed, while the fisherman picks up the rod to set the hook.

Rigging for Big Game

Perhaps the most challenging form of salt-water fishing for both the boatman and angler is the pursuit of big game fish —marlin, tuna, sailfish, shark and swordfish. Pacific marlin occasionally weigh in at half a ton, and can run with a hook in bursts of speed of up to 20 knots. The record white shark, caught off Ceduna, Australia, in 1959, weighed an astonishing 2,664 pounds.

The stalking of these giants may carry a fisherman as much as 60 miles offshore. And though stretches of deep water and warm ocean currents near the shores of Florida and the Bahamas bring the big ones within striking distance of small day cruisers, in other areas a sturdy, ocean-going craft with deepwater cruising capability is essential.

Aboard any deepwater fishing boat, special equipment and techniques for trolling are employed to aid in the search and capture. The larger boats are fitted with outriggers, sturdy metal or fiberglass poles 15 to 35 feet long, set into holders along the gunwales. These outriggers act as extensions of the fisherman's rods. When lowered to an angle of approximately 45° outboard, they troll the baits outside the boat's wake without danger of entangling the multiple lines that a deep-sea vessel ordinarily sets. A hard strike automatically frees the line from the outrigger *(left, below)*. Some big game anglers, when trolling particularly shallow offshore banks, or when fishing from small boats not equipped with outriggers, clip their lines to a kite *(right)*.

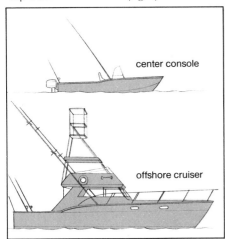

Among the craft generally used for offshore trolling are the 22-foot center-console outboard at top and the 44-foot cruiser below it, equipped with tuna tower and outriggers. The smaller boat, popular in tropical waters, is ideal for trolling up to 40 miles offshore. With the larger vessel, a fisherman can extend his range to over 60 miles offshore, and can remain at sea for several days at a time.

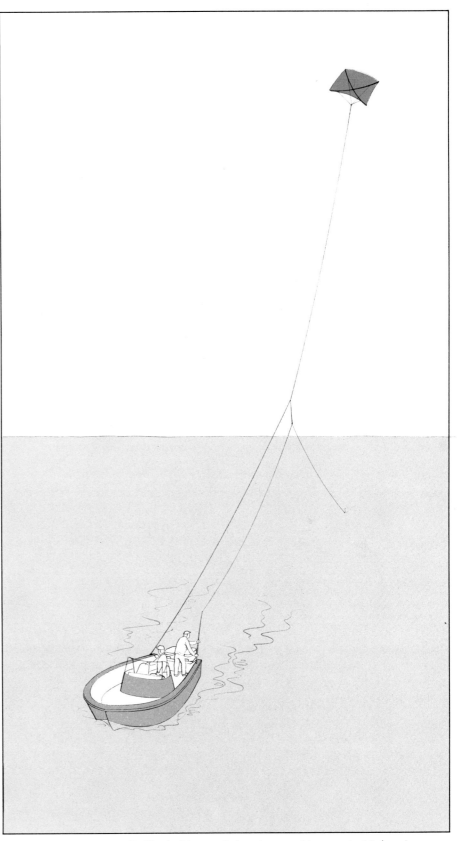

Trolling by kite, a technique borrowed from ancient Polynesian fishermen, increases an angler's control over his lure. The fisherman attaches his line to the string of a fair-sized nylon kite with an outrigger spring clip. The angler pays out both kite string and fishing line as the kite is sent aloft; the clip releases when a fish strikes the bait hard. With this rig, the fisherman can work the fishing line and kite string to place the bait over a likely fishing spot —even to lift it out of the water. This action not only entices reluctant game fish, but helps keep bait away from unwanted fish.

A lookout's lofty perch atop a 30-foot tuna tower not only increases his chances of spotting the protruding fin of a game fish; or the splash of a school of jumping baitfish, but also of catching a glimpse of game fish swimming beneath the surface. Because refraction turns the surface of the water into a mirror image of the sky when the viewer's sight line is less than 20° from the horizontal, the underwater vision of a fisherman on a flying bridge is limited to a circle with a radius of approximately 40 feet on an ordinary craft. But the effective fish-spotting radius of a man atop a tower is twice as large.

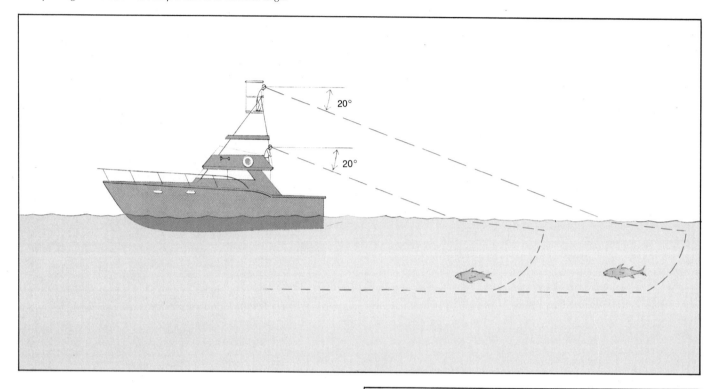

To search for a fish that has sounded, a skipper drops a floating mark at the spot where the fish was last seen and begins to work a search pattern around it. First he runs away from the mark for one minute at a steady five-knot trolling speed, then turns 90° right for another one-minute run. He continues this spiral pattern, extending his time to two minutes for the next two consecutive legs, then two three-minute legs—all the while sweeping larger areas of water. After completing two four-minute runs, the skipper finishes off the pattern with a five-minute run, then alters course to the right to retrieve the flag.

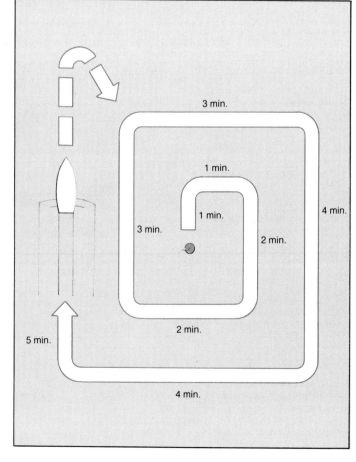

Angling for a Strike

To many deepwater anglers, the most exciting moments come when a big game fish is sighted and first strikes the bait. Unlike fresh-water and inshore bottom fishing, in which the angler is essentially on his own, the big game fisherman is only one member of a tightly coordinated team. For example, it takes a practiced eye in the tower to spot a solitary marlin or swordfish lazing just under the surface on a choppy day. Once spotted, the fish may duck below the surface, or sound, and only a skillful hand on the helm can run a tight search pattern that will bring the baits close to the fish—and then coax the fish to strike.

The instant of the strike is particularly tense, requiring precise timing *(right)* between skipper and angler. The angler immediately jumps into the fighting chair, while the skipper readies himself for a series of maneuvers that might make a tight landing at a crowded marina look like child's play. Throughout the fight the fish must be outmaneuvered *(overleaf)*, particularly to prevent it from snapping the line with a sudden leap or turn. Quick work at the helm is especially important to the conservation-minded sportsman who wants to return his fish to the sea after winning the battle, for a game fish that has been on the hook for long may be too exhausted to survive.

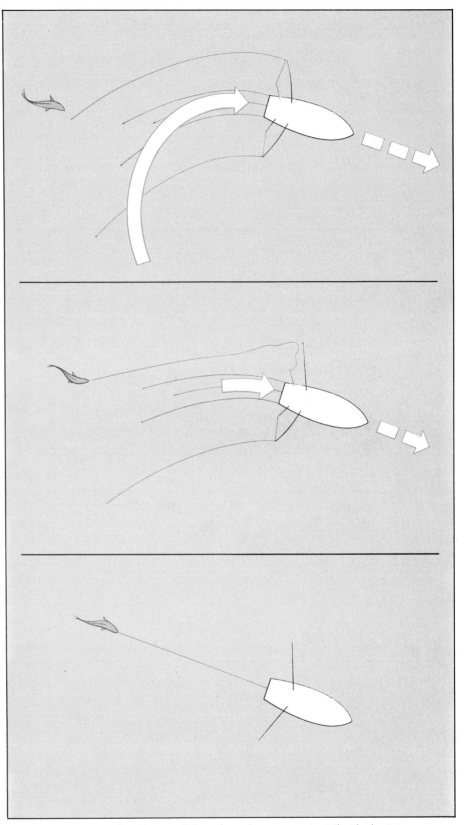

As a big game fish on the surface prepares to strike, the boatman turns carefully away from the fish (top) so that it will be presented with only one of the baits; this prevents the fish from becoming distracted by the other lines. When the fish strikes this proffered bait, the outrigger clip releases and spills the line into the water (center). The skipper quickly puts the engine in neutral so as not to pull the bait from the fish's mouth. Then, as the angler sets the hook, the crewmen retrieve any other trolling lines (bottom).

After a game fish takes the bait, it nearly always makes a sudden frenzied charge in one of the six basic directions represented by the arrows below; the boatman and fisherman must respond with the appropriate set of maneuvers, as illustrated below and on the opposite page. First, when the fish strikes, the fisherman pauses a moment to make sure that the fish has been firmly hooked. Then, depending on the direction the fish takes, the fisherman takes in slack or eases it out, while the boatman steers to help compensate for the fish's advantage in both weight and strength over his antagonist.

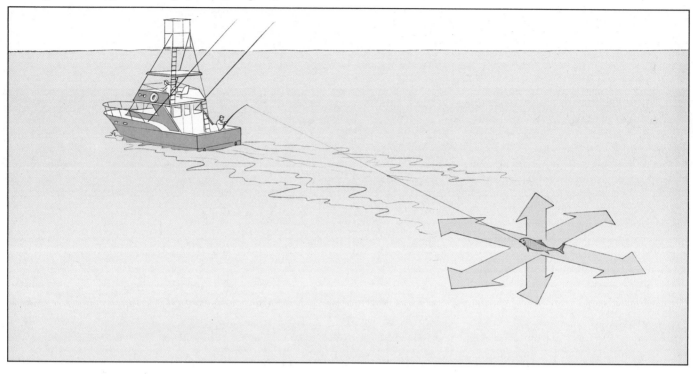

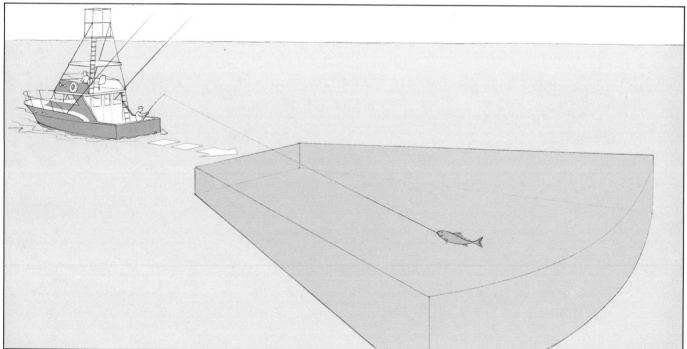

After the fish has expended some of its initial energy, the fisherman can begin to guide it into position for reeling in and gaffing. Ideally, this position will be within a wedge-shaped zone extending 100 yards aft of the boat. Once the quarry has been worked into this area, it may begin to swim toward the boat, in which case the boatman eases forward to help take up slack in the water. More often, however, the skipper gently reverses at a rate sufficient to keep the line taut but to lighten strain on the fisherman's arms as he reels in. By use of this latter method, one fisherman boated a 500-pound tuna in 12 minutes.

If the fish charges rapidly away from the boat, the skipper must turn his craft and give chase—but at a course about 30° off that of the fish, in order to avoid snagging or running over the line (below, left). From this position the skipper carefully watches the fish to be sure it does not turn and cross his bow, which would also entangle the line. If the fish does turn, the boatman must turn with him (below), and then continue to swing away from the fish, opening the angle and at the same time gunning ahead to pull out the long curve that has developed in the line during the maneuver.

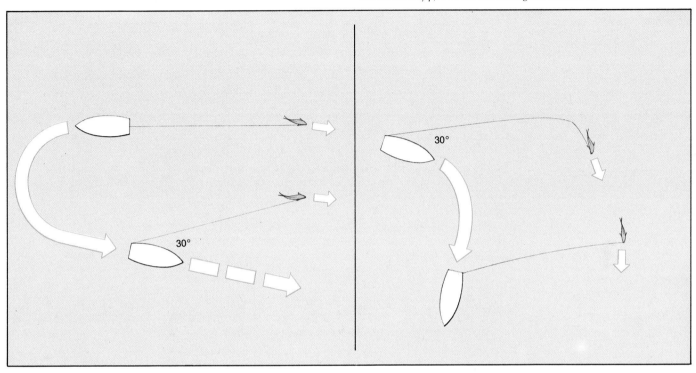

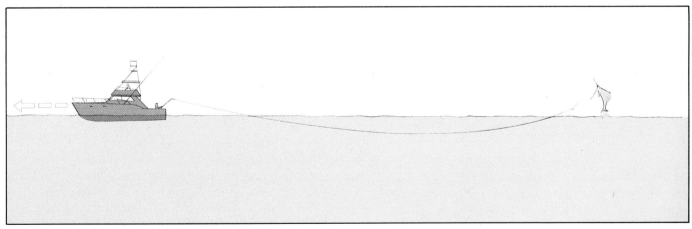

Acrobatic fighters like sailfish often try to throw a lure from their mouths by leaping high into the air. Even if the fish cannot shake the lure, his leaps put slack in the line. And if the fish, falling back into the water, hits the slack line, the line is liable to break. To minimize this risk, the fisherman allows the fish to take slack off the reel during the initial stage of a jump, easing strain on the line. Meanwhile, the skipper moves the boat ahead to take up slack as the fish descends.

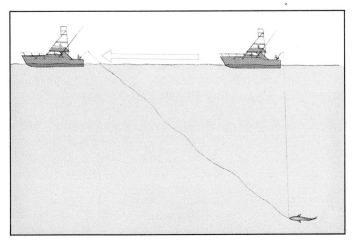

In the fight's final stages, the fish often sounds and rolls over on its side, making it nearly impossible to reel it to the surface. To break the stalemate, a fisherman pulls hard on the line to accustom the fish to pressure on its mouth, then lets the line go slack as the skipper eases ahead. The fish, believing the line has broken, begins to swim away and can then be coaxed into the ideal landing zone (opposite).

Working as a team, the fisherman and the crewman at right prepare to boat an albacore of 60 or so pounds, which can be hauled aboard with a gaff. The fisherman, wearing leather-reinforced gloves for protection, pulls hard on the leader to keep the fish close alongside. The crewman slips the hook of the gaff under the fish's pectoral fin, quickly jerks the sharp point into the soft flesh of the fish's belly and hauls the catch aboard.

Tail-roping a fish of 100 or more pounds requires the fisherman to hold the leader momentarily taut while a crewman (right) loops a stout line around the leader, quickly forms a large noose by tying a slipknot and then slides the noose down the fish's body to cinch it tightly around the tail. (The fish's tail is so active and dangerous that it cannot be simply tied at the outset.) The crewman attaches the line to a hook at the bottom of a block and tackle suspended from a gin pole —a 12-foot davit-like crane. The fisherman can then join the crewman (bottom right) in heaving the fish up and into the boat.

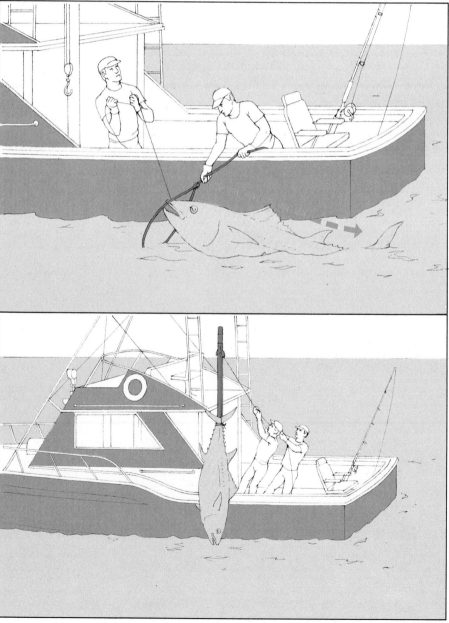

Bringing a Fish Aboard

Though medium-sized ocean game fish can be hauled aboard a boat with no more than a gaff, more sophisticated techniques must be employed when boating a fish weighing several hundred pounds. This is especially true of a big fish that is still full of fight after having been brought alongside. The best way of handling such a formidable catch is to get a loop of rope around the fish's thrashing tail—its source of power—(center left) and then lift it with a block and tackle mounted on a so-called gin pole (bottom left).

A growing trend among sportsmen today, however, is to release big game fish after bringing them to boat. A fisherman who does not intend to keep his catch will sometimes detain it just long enough to tag it. Government and private agencies such as the National Marine Fisheries Service and the International Game Fish Association, which study the migration of game fish, supply fishermen with special numbered tags (right). The fisherman affixes the tag, as shown at right below, and then releases the fish. Sport or commercial fishermen who recapture a tagged fish are urged to report to the issuing agency the number of the tag and such data as the place and date of the capture.

A dart-tagger for marking game fish to be released is much like a harpoon. Its detachable head is a razor-sharp metal dart that fits loosely over a spike protruding from the shaft. One end of a length of wire sheathed in plastic is attached to the dart. At the other end of the wire is a plastic cylinder—held to the harpoon shaft with a rubber band—that is embossed with a tag number and instructions for reporting the catch. After tagging the fish, the fisherman records its species, sex and estimated weight on a card bearing the number of the tag, and sends this information to the tag-issuing agency.

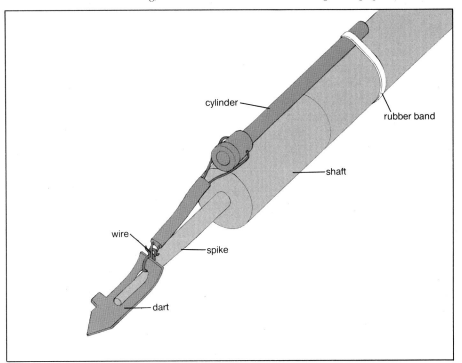

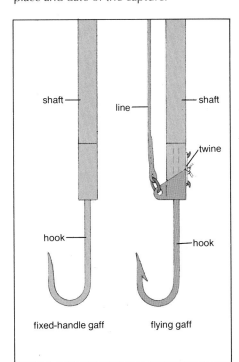

Above are the two main types of ocean-fishing gaffs. A fixed-handle gaff (left) has a steel hook set in the end of a wooden shaft. A flying gaff has a detachable hook with a ring and a stout line. This hook assembly is temporarily bound to its shaft with light twine. Once the hook is firmly in the fish, the twine breaks and the pole and hook pull apart. The fish is then hauled in by the line.

An angler controlling a fish for tagging holds the leader tightly in his gloved hands—as he would if he and the crewman were gaffing or tail-roping their catch. Meanwhile, the crewman plunges the tagging dart into the fish's flesh alongside the dorsal fin. Insertion of the dart does not hurt the fish, and the wound caused by the dart, which remains embedded in the fish's flesh, soon heals. When the tagger draws back the harpoon, the tag pulls loose from the rubber band holding it to the shaft. At the same time, the fisherman cuts the leader with a pair of clippers and sets the fish free.

Finalists board a chartered DC-8 bound for the unannounced site of the BASS Masters Classic.

FRIENDLY FRACAS FOR A MESS OF FISH

Perhaps only in feisty, get-ahead America could an essentially sedentary recreation like fishing be turned into a competitive sport. The essential form of fishing combat is the tournament, and hundreds of these contests are held annually throughout the country. They range from small-town shad derbies that last a single day to the Metropolitan South Florida Fishing Tournament, which runs for months and covers 34 species of fish in eight tackle divisions.

Some end with the quarry being consumed in fish fries, others with proud anglers posed beside the suspended bodies of their vanquished prey. But the growing trend in these preservation-conscious times is toward releasing the fish as soon as the catch has been recorded. Indeed, no fish are even hoisted aboard boats in the most prestigious of all big-game-fish tournaments, the Masters Invitational Billfish Tournament, held each January in Palm Beach, Florida. Anglers use special barbless hooks as an extra challenge to their skill, and points are awarded for the speed with which sailfish are reeled in before being released.

Prizes are as varied as the tournaments. The Masters winner takes home a pair of book ends and a copy of Ernest Hemingway's *The Old Man and the Sea*. Other contests involve thousands of dollars in cash prizes. Oddly, the fish that brings the biggest money to the conquering angler is one of the smaller of those avidly sought by U.S. fishermen, namely, the black bass. The size of the payoff reflects both the large numbers of bass fishermen and their esteem for this diminutive battler. The sportsman and novelist Zane Grey, whose views have the weight of Holy Writ among fishermen, has said black bass are the "most beautiful and gamy fish that swim."

The pinnacle of bass competition and thus the Super Bowl of all fishing tournaments is the BASS Masters Classic, held each fall—after a full season of qualifying rounds—by the Bass Anglers Sportsman Society (BASS, for short), whose emblem is depicted at left.

Since the ultimate test of a bass fisherman is how quickly he can figure out where the fish will bite in water he has never seen before, the site of each year's Classic is kept a closely guarded secret until the last possible moment. Even the location of the airport at which the 26 finalists are told to assemble offers no clue. The tournament grounds may be hours away from the take-off point—or only minutes. Not until the contestants are airborne is their destination revealed.

Those taking part in the Classic pictured on these and the following pages met in New Orleans and were flown to man-made Clark Hill Lake on the Georgia-South Carolina border. There they were given one day to reconnoiter the 70,000-acre lake for so-called honey holes, the underwater hideouts where the greatest numbers of hungry bass may lurk.

Then for the next three days they fished eight hours a day from identical bass boats that had been trucked to the lake from Arkansas secretly and by night. The rules limited each day's catch to 10 fish —none of them under 12 inches—and awarded a one-ounce bonus for every bass brought in alive in the boats' aerated live wells. An official observer rode in each boat to thwart such shenanigans as enhancing the weight of a fish with a bellyful of bird shot. After all the bass had been weighed and released, the angler with the highest three-day total was officially canonized as the best bass fisherman in the U.S.—which, to any self-respecting bass catcher, means the best fisherman of any kind in the whole world.

BASS contestants and observers man their 16-foot, swivel-seated bass boats in the predawn chilliness just before the start of a day's fishing.

Contestants jockey their craft into line as they await the signal flare that will start the fishing competition. Each of the 26 entrants had spent the previous day test fishing the lake for the most likely spots, and each was now aiming to get to the choice holes first.

Just after the starting signal, the fleet of bass boats, powered by 85-horsepower outboard engines, blasts off in clouds of spray and exhaust fumes. Once on the fishing grounds, anglers used quiet, low-powered electric motors, mounted on the bows of the boats, to slowly maneuver their craft.

A fisherman holds a bass hooked on a spinner-type lure. Once the hook is out, the fish, still kicking, will be put into the boat's aerated live well for weighing at day's end.

Standing in the bow of his boat, a contestant retrieves his line after a cast while his seated observer passes the time by trying to catch a fish of his own—usually a fruitless pursuit. "Throwing a line in the water a pro has worked," admitted one observer, "is like fishing behind a vacuum cleaner."

An angler tries his luck amid a stand of dead trees, which were drowned by rising waters when a dam constructed across the Savannah River created Clark Hill Lake in 1955. Tournament boats are carpeted throughout their interiors to muffle sound, and are also equipped with electric anchor winches, depth finders and devices for measuring the water's oxygen content and temperature.

A plastic bag bulging with bass weighs in at 24 pounds 11 ounces on the official scales. This hefty haul gave the second-day lead to Rayo Breckenridge (right), a cotton-and-soybean farmer from Arkansas. It proved to be the best single day's catch of the contest.

A marine biologist helps a fish to recover from the ordeals of being hooked, bagged and weighed by pulling it gently through oxygenated water in a 525-gallon tank. The water also contains acriflavin, which kills any bacteria the fish might have acquired from being handled. BASS officials estimate that 85 per cent of the fish caught during their tournaments live to be fished for again.

With the final results of the competition in, a three-day total catch of 52 pounds 8 ounces gave the trophy—and also $15,000—to Breckenridge.

3 Back inshore from the broad rivers, lakes and coastal haunts of most sail- and powerboats lies an enormous lacework of interior waterways that serves as a frontier for a special breed of inland skippers. These latter-day explorers pilot light, highly maneuverable boats with shallow drafts and resilient hulls that allow their owners to travel into fresh-water ponds and rocky, stream-fed rivers that are inaccessible to conventional boats. The craft that most boatmen use for navigating in these all but landlocked waters is the canoe, a direct descendant of the birchbark vessels that were developed centuries ago by the American Indians *(page 90)*. Propelled by the strokes of one or two

BACK-COUNTRY BOATING

paddlers, canoes can glide delicately over calm water, yet they prove themselves to be surprisingly stable, seaworthy and maneuverable, even in rapids like those pictured at left. Early European adventurers so marveled at canoeborne Indians, who paddled circles around their ships' bulky longboats, that they quickly adopted bark boats in order to explore the forests of the northeast, and to ply fur-trading routes spanning half the continent.

Canoe cruising became popular as a sport in the mid-1800s, when city dwellers sought escape in travel down scenic and unspoiled waterways. Such literary backwoodsmen as Henry David Thoreau hired Indian guides to take them through the woods of Maine, Minnesota and Ontario in birchbark canoes, and brought back accounts that stirred the imagination of a whole generation of leisure-seeking Americans. In England, where no suitable bark was available, bands of enterprising paddlers from the Royal Canoe Club logged cruises on the Thames in canoes that were fashioned from tin and from India rubber with air cells in the bow and stern. In 1873, a former shoe clerk, Henry Rushton, opened a small factory to build wooden canoes in Canton, New York. Within the decade after the start of Rushton's factory, scores of canoe clubs had sprung up throughout the nation; the members of these new clubs were dedicated to convivial and sometimes heroically ambitious voyaging. A team of New Yorkers in two wooden canoes, for example, started an eight-month trip in 1882 that ultimately took them some 3,800 miles, from Lake George through the Erie Canal and down the Allegheny and Mississippi rivers all the way to the Gulf of Mexico.

The past dozen years have seen a renewed interest in canoeing—which was spurred by a second revolution in construction materials. Today more than two million paddlers annually take canoe trips on wilderness lakes and rivers. Moreover, it is not necessary to own a canoe in order to embark on such adventures. Hundreds of commercial outfitters, usually situated near popularly canoed rivers like the upper Delaware in New York, the Shenandoah in Virginia or the Buffalo in Arkansas, rent canoes, paddles and life jackets for day trips or for overnight cruises.

The most challenging of the nation's rivers, such as the turbulent Salmon in Idaho, the Rogue in Oregon, and sections of the steep and lively West River in Vermont, are too hazardous for the standard variety of canoe. Instead, these cascading streams are invaded each spring and summer by white-water specialists who are willing to dare the worst rapids in other types of carefully adapted craft. These include watertight kayaks, decked-over competition canoes, rowing dories and inflatable rubber rafts that are used to plunge down rivers like the Colorado and the Snake. The larger boats stay out on cruising trips that may last as long as three weeks. The swift kayaks and specialized canoes enter slalom races that take no more than a few minutes to complete *(pages 114-115)*—but may have an Olympic gold medal waiting at the end of the final pitch of churning water.

Two canoeists thread their craft through a rocky 14-mile-long stretch of rapids during an early summer voyage down the blue waters of the Dead River in Maine.

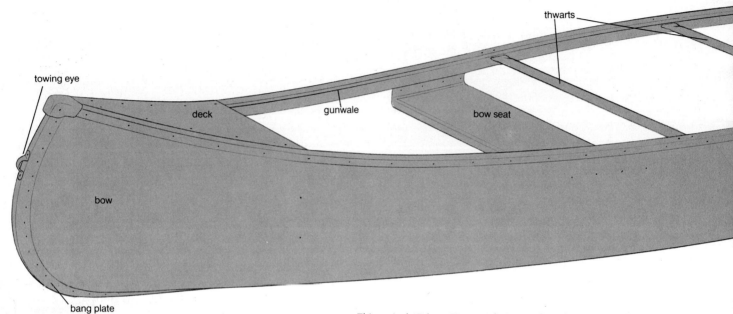

This typical 17-foot, 75-pound canoe is broad-beamed and essentially flat-bottomed to provide both stability and cargo space. Its sharply tapered bow and stern are designed to knife cleanly through lake and river waters. Horizontal thwarts add structural strength to the hull, as do the seats attached fore and aft. Gunwales running the length of the boat and small triangular decks at the slightly upswept bow and stern provide additional stiffening. So-called bang plates reinforce the stem and the stern against damage from collisions with rocks. A towing eye at the bow provides an attachment for a painter.

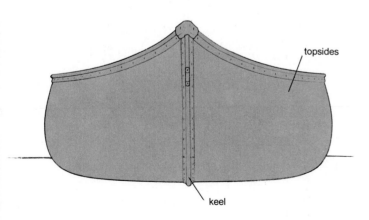

This view from the bow shows the shallow draft of a canoe under normal loads. The topsides curve sharply at the waterline, giving the craft a maximum amount of freeboard; the tumble home at the gunwale line helps keep cargo and passengers dry. A small keel, running from stem to stern, helps keep the craft on a straight course through open stretches of water. Canoes built especially for shooting rapids lack keels, so that the craft can turn more quickly.

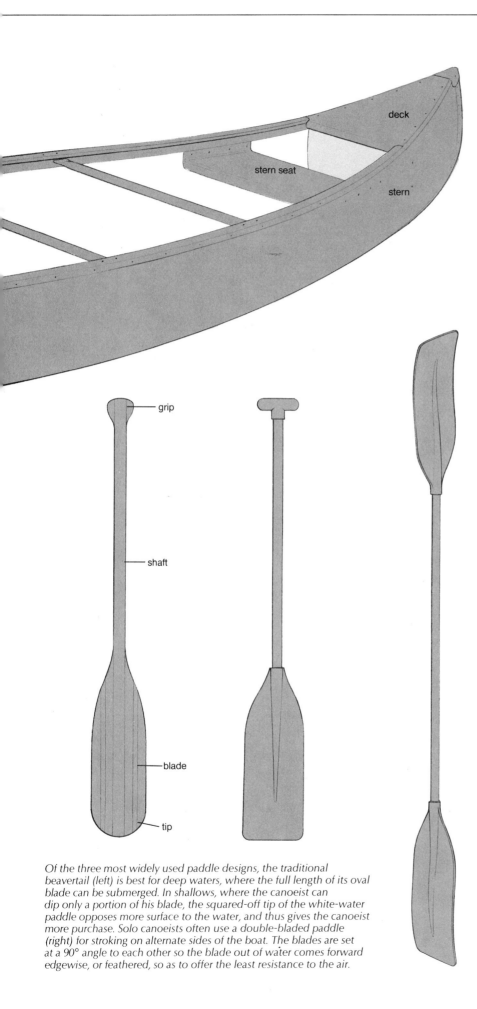

The Versatile Canoe

The graceful lines of a modern sport canoe like the one at left are essentially those of the supremely functional birchbark craft developed by the American Indians. These versatile double-enders were used to fish on lakes and streams, to hunt wild fowl in shallow marshes, or to carry heavy loads of goods and people over long distances. Though sturdy enough for such heavy-duty work, they were at the same time lightweight for ease in paddling and for carrying around rapids and waterfalls. In addition, they were highly maneuverable, relatively stable in rough water and buoyant enough to float even when swamped. No boat ever invented better served its purpose.

Modern canoes embody all the virtues of the ancestral craft—plus the extra strength and lightness of modern structural materials. The one shown here is of aluminum; plastic, fiberglass and wood laminates *(overleaf)* are also widely used. Modern canoes range in size from diminutive 12-footers used by solitary fishermen to ones of 22 or more feet that can carry three people and a month's provisions. Two voyagers of average ability can paddle one of these craft up to 25 miles in a day without undue effort. And most canoes can be hauled up on a beach, loaded onto and off-loaded from a cartop, or even portaged for one or two miles by a single person.

Paddles, like the canoes themselves, are of Indian ancestry. Modern ones are made of fiberglass, plastic—or laminations combining hardwoods for strength with softwoods for lightness. Even these tough implements, however, have been known to break. And a voyager who lacks the skill to use knife and ax to fashion a replacement out of spruce—as did the Indians—is well advised not to go up the creek without a spare.

Of the three most widely used paddle designs, the traditional beavertail (left) is best for deep waters, where the full length of its oval blade can be submerged. In shallows, where the canoeist can dip only a portion of his blade, the squared-off tip of the white-water paddle opposes more surface to the water, and thus gives the canoeist more purchase. Solo canoeists often use a double-bladed paddle (right) for stroking on alternate sides of the boat. The blades are set at a 90° angle to each other so the blade out of water comes forward edgewise, or feathered, so as to offer the least resistance to the air.

The Canoe's Anatomy

Among the 150,000 canoes sold annually in the United States, aluminum craft are by far the most popular. They require little maintenance beyond decorative painting and can endure prolonged outdoor exposure. Moreover, aluminum is flexible, taking nothing worse from a normal bump than an easily hammered-out dent.

Fiberglass hulls are more resilient, rebounding unscathed from collisions. And though they are more likely to crack or rupture, they are easily repaired with an application of cloth and resin. They need occasional cleaning and some protection from the elements when in storage.

Plastic canoes, introduced in the late 1960s, bounce off most rocks without denting or cracking, but if damaged they are harder to repair than fiberglass. Their ultimate life spans have yet to be determined; but as a measure of durability, test models have survived being thrown from atop five-story buildings.

Wood and canvas canoes are the heaviest, costliest and most elegant. Minor damage to their outer skin is mendable, but a bad collision with a rock can necessitate new ribs and planks. And wood craft require periodic scraping, painting and varnishing, and need protected storage.

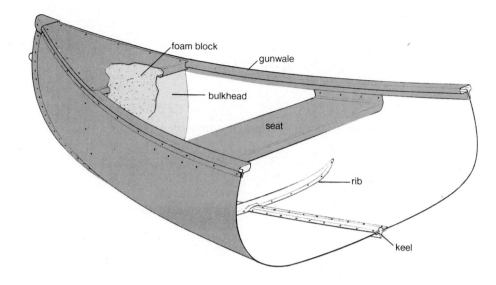

This aluminum canoe is made by riveting together half-hull sections stamped from aluminum-alloy sheets. The hull is strengthened by an aluminum keel running the length of the boat's underside, and by ribs riveted across the inside of the bottom. Seats are riveted in place for additional structural strength. Blocks of foam-flotation material set behind aluminum bulkheads at the bow and stern provide buoyancy.

The Indian Way

This birchbark canoe is taking shape in 1901 under the hands of a family of northern Minnesota Chippewa Indians. They are using traditional methods and materials developed by north-woods Indians long before the first white explorers arrived, and communicated from tribe to tribe across the continent.

These shipwrights first outlined the shape of the canoe with stakes driven into the ground. Inside the enclosure they placed a length of bark stripped from the trunk of a paper birch. The bark was held in place between the stakes by smooth river-bed stones. The builders lashed gunwales to the upper edge of the bark, as shown at left. They then set steam-bent cedar ribs at two-inch intervals along the bark's inner surface and used split spruce roots to stitch the bark to the completed frame. Finally, they sealed all seams below the waterline with spruce gum.

The result of two weeks of labor was a stout and stable vessel like the craft of the legendary Hiawatha, which the poet Henry Longfellow described as having "floated on the river like a yellow leaf in autumn, like a yellow water lily." So handy and effective was the birchbark, in fact, that the French in 1750 set up the world's first canoe factory on the banks of the St. Lawrence River, with a production rate of 20 boats a year.

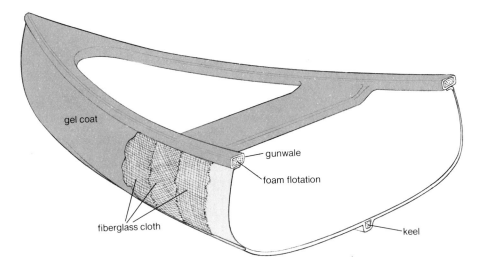

A typical fiberglass canoe is formed in a concave mold that is first sprayed inside with a colored plastic. This so-called gel coat becomes a decorative outer skin for the boat. Sheets of fiberglass cloth are then laid up within the mold and impregnated with resin to create a hull so strong that it needs no reinforcing ribs. Expandable foam, injected into the boat's hollow gunwales and keel, makes it unsinkable. Some fiberglass hulls outweigh those of aluminum or plastic, but others made with a synthetic cloth called Kevlar are lighter and equally strong.

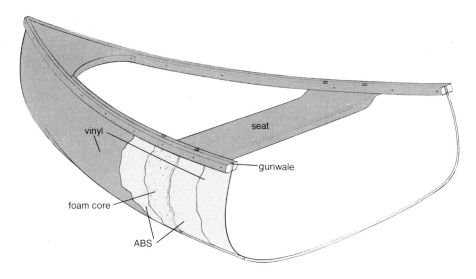

A plastic canoe hull is produced in one swift, simple operation out of a rigid thermoplastic, which consists of a foam core sandwiched between multiple layers of vinyl and acrylonitrile-butadiene-styrene (ABS). A sheet of this material is placed in a vacuum chamber, heated, then sucked into shape around a hull mold. The foam core provides buoyancy. The hull here has been made without a keel for use in rapids; those intended for calmer waters are made from molds with keels. The seats, also made from thermoplastic, are bolted to the gunwales.

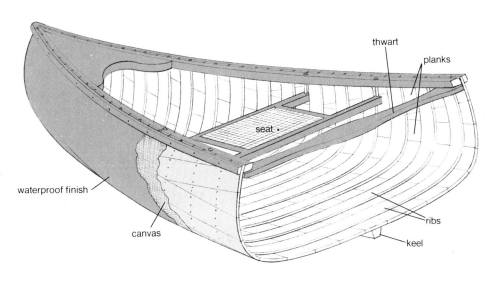

The frame of a typical hand-crafted wood-and-canvas canoe is built up from U-shaped cedar ribs three-eighths inch thick and three inches wide, spaced two inches or so apart. Thin spruce or cedar planks are secured to this skeleton with copper fastenings. The planks are covered with a seamless skin of cloth—either traditional cotton canvas, or tougher and less-moisture-absorbent Dacron. Subsequently the fabric is waterproofed with a hard-drying filler and painted. A metal-shod wooden keel protects the bottom of the boat from scrapes. The addition of wooden seats and thwarts completes the classic look.

Rigged for sailing, this double-ended canoe's accessory equipment is almost entirely detachable. The removable aluminum mast that supports the sail and its rigging rests on a mast step permanently bolted to a clip in the bilge, and is held firmly upright by a mast thwart affixed to the gunwales. The hardwood leeboards are secured to a spreader bar clamped to the gunwales. The aluminum rudder and steering bar are fixed to a curved mount that is bolted to the stern.

lateen sail

boom

mast

mast thwart

mast step

spreader bar

steering lines

steering bar

leeboard

rudder

Canoe Conversions

An ordinary canoe can quickly be transformed into an efficient sailboat, rowboat or powerboat using the equipment shown here. For example, in a matter of minutes, an ingenious factory-prepared kit like the one at left converts a canoe into a day sailer very much like the light, graceful sailing canoes that enjoyed a considerable fad among United States boatmen at the turn of the century. Not intended for heavy weather, such sailing rigs are surprisingly stable in light to medium breezes, and on certain specialized canoes produce speeds of up to 16 knots.

Less glamorous, but practical either for upstream travel or for fishing in fast water —where paddling is insufficient to counter the current—is a rowing kit. Most canoes are too narrow for good rowing leverage with gunwale-mounted oarlocks. The kit's seat has an oarlock extension to allow the oars to be properly mounted.

Small gas- and electric-powered outboard motors, ranging from 2 to 5 horsepower and from 10 to 50 pounds, are helpful on long hauls, in rough water and for trolling. Motors like those below are side-mounted on double-ended canoes, or rear-mounted on flat transoms.

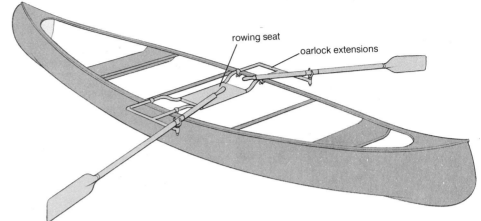

This simple but efficient rowing unit consists of a combination seat-and-oarlock extension that clamps to the gunwales. It provides about four feet between oarlocks, enough for a rower to position a pair of seven-foot oars, as shown, for maximum leverage on each stroke.

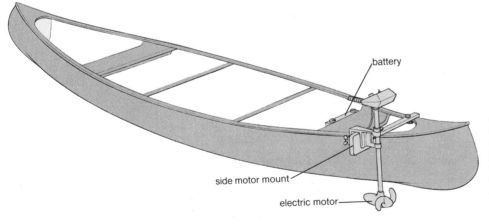

A popular trolling rig for canoes is a small electric outboard motor like this two-horsepower unit fastened to the after gunwales with a clamp-on side motor mount. Powered by a 12- or 24-volt battery, the electric motor can move the canoe almost silently at three knots for up to four hours.

Canoe campers or fishermen who move heavy loads long distances sometimes use a gas-powered outboard motor of two to five horsepower mounted on a squared-off stern. Although a skilled craftsman can square off a double-ender, most gas-outboard users buy a squared stern to begin with. Such models can also be paddled, but then they do not balance as well as double-enders.

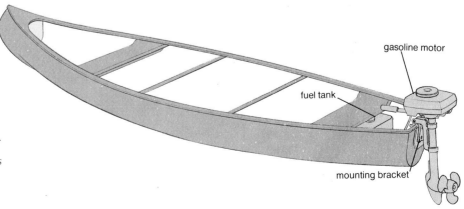

First Steps in Canoeing

Though canoes have a reputation for in-stability, they are actually among the steadiest of small boats—as long as passengers and gear are properly arranged aboard. The guiding principle is to keep the weight low in the boat, and evenly distributed. This not only enhances the stability of the craft, but also helps to maintain proper trim. In lake paddling, the canoe should be level or slightly down by the stern under normal conditions; with a crosswind it should be an inch or two down by the bow to help keep the breeze from blowing it off course. When moving in white water, the canoe should always be level to allow the stern to swing quickly in avoiding rocks. In all cases, the gear should be balanced along the canoe's centerline, and lashed down securely.

One way to keep weight low in the canoe is for all hands aboard to avoid standing up—although an exception to that rule occurs when poling (pages 98-99). Canoeists should crouch low when boarding and when shifting position afloat. During any such movements, grasping the gunwales on both sides (right) not only helps balance the canoeist, but also steadies the craft by spreading weight athwartships.

A lone paddler generally places himself as close to amidships as possible. Alone or in tandem, paddlers can lower their weight and increase stability by kneeling in the bottom of the canoe instead of taking a seat—a good precaution in rough waters. In stroking (pages 96-97), they should synchronize their movements to maintain balance; pulling their paddles through the water with smooth, rhythmic motions; for a graceful, splash-free recovery, they should feather their paddles, turning the tips of the blades parallel to the surface of the water when bringing them back to begin a new stroke.

Boarding a canoe that is lying parallel to a pier, the canoeist stoops, grips the gunwales amidships with both hands, and places one foot on the craft's centerline, keeping the other foot on the pier. Once he has the boat firmly in hand, he will transfer his weight to the foot in the boat and then bring in the other foot. The paddle should always be put aboard before the canoeist steps on, since the craft may begin to float away from the pier as the boatman settles himself.

Launching from the shore, two canoeists position their craft at right angles to the water's edge, stern facing out, with the bow slightly aground. One person steps aboard at the centerline—leaning low and sliding his hands along the gunwales—while a companion steadies the bow. The boarder moves quickly to the stern, turns around and sits down. Then the second man shoves the canoe away from the beach, wades into the water, grasps the gunwales and steps aboard. He must be careful to maintain a low crouch while turning around and seating himself.

Paddling in tandem, these two canoeists have
distributed their weight for optimum stability
and trim—the smaller one in the bow,
the larger in the stern, with their gear lashed
down amidships. Besides this correct fore-and-
aft trim, they balance the canoe laterally by
stroking on opposite sides, a maneuver that
will also serve to keep the craft moving ahead
along a straight course. The bow paddler's
primary job is to pull steadily, straight ahead,
while the one in the stern has the added
responsibility of steering (overleaf).

A solitary canoeist kneels aft of the center
thwart, his gear lashed down in front to
balance his weight. When wielding a double-
bladed paddle, as here, he uses alternate
port and starboard strokes to stay on course.

The basic method for moving a canoe forward is the straight pulling stroke. Paddling to starboard, the canoeist cradles the paddle's grip in her left hand, and clasps the shaft just above the blade with her right hand. Reaching forward with both arms, she digs the paddle into the water until the blade is two-thirds submerged. Then she pushes forward with her left arm while pulling back (arrow) with her right. When the paddle is just past her hip, she lifts it out of the water.

The reverse stroke can slow or stop a canoe's forward motion, or move it backward. To perform it, the canoeist holds the paddle close to his body, with the blade at right angles to the boat. Keeping the shaft vertical, he thrusts the blade into the water. He then pushes forward (arrow) with his right hand, while keeping a slight backward pressure with his left hand. In completing the stroke, he extends both arms forward as far as he can reach before feathering back.

The J stroke, executed by the stern paddler, counters the tendency of a canoe to swerve away from the side on which it is being paddled. At the end of a normal pulling stroke, the canoeist keeps the blade in the water but turns it parallel to the boat's side. She then pushes the submerged paddle away from the canoe with an outward thrust (arrow) of her right hand. This swings the bow back on course.

A forward sweep stroke, executed from the bow, changes the path of the canoe, pointing the boat away from the side on which the canoeist is paddling. To initiate the stroke, the paddler extends his right arm forward as far as possible, dipping the paddle into the water at a 45° angle. With the blade just beneath the water's surface, he pulls it outward (arrow) and back through a 90° arc. This stroke is useful for making gradual changes in course in open water.

A draw stroke, essential for making quick turns in rocky rivers, pulls the canoe toward the side on which a person is paddling. Holding the blade parallel to the canoe, the canoeist—either at stern (as here) or bow—reaches out at right angles and plunges the paddle vertically into the water. Then she quickly draws the blade toward her (dark arrow), thus moving the canoe toward the paddle (light arrow).

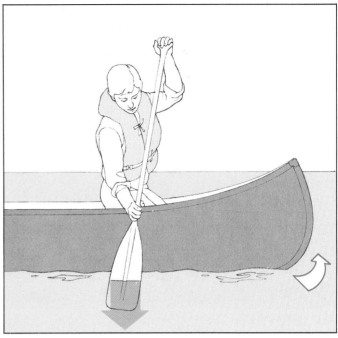

The pry stroke is the direct opposite of the draw. In it, the canoeist jabs the paddle into the water, the blade facing the side of the boat, then pushes it quickly outward (dark arrow). The canoe responds by turning away (light arrow) from the direction of the push.

Using her paddle like a rudder, the stern paddler can steer a moving craft without any need for stroking. The canoeist holds the paddle rigidly in the water, its trailing edge angled slightly outward. The stern will gradually swerve (light arrow) toward the side in which the paddle is held. Like the J stroke, the stern rudder provides the canoeist with an effective method for offsetting the tendency of a canoe to veer off course from continuous stroking on one side.

The bow rudder is an emergency action used by some canoeists to draw a rapidly moving canoe away from an obstacle ahead. The bow-man drives his paddle into the water with the blade's trailing edge angled outward at about 30°, and holds it firmly in position. The canoe swerves (light arrow)—and also slows its forward motion.

Techniques for Poling

Many rivers are too fast-moving or too shallow for paddling—especially when the canoeist is trying to make his way upstream. To give himself the needed power for upstream work, or to slow his boat while heading downstream, the canoeist can employ one of the oldest known methods of propelling a boat: poling. (The same basic technique is used in calm, shallow water to guide certain specialized fishing boats, as illustrated on page 63.)

The poler is the sternman and must begin by disregarding the canoeist's caveat never to stand up while underway; to properly handle the pole, which is 12 to 14 feet long and made of aluminum or iron-tipped wood or fiberglass, he must stand erect. To get into the proper poling stance, the sternman simply rises from his seat in one smooth motion to stand with his knees comfortably flexed to absorb the motion of the canoe. One foot—the left foot for a right-handed canoeist—should be placed just forward of the stern seat and slightly to one side of the canoe's centerline; the other should be set diagonally forward on the opposite side near the after thwart. The canoeist is thus in a firm, balanced stance with a clear view forward but with his legs opened to an angle of about 45° toward the side of the boat on which he will be poling.

When bucking the current, the canoeist plunges the pole into the water close to the gunwale, and then pushes with it in a rhythmic, hand-over-hand motion *(top row at right)*. He heads the canoe through sections of shallow but unobstructed water, where the shallow bottom tends to cut the current's force and makes for easy setting of the pole. When going downstream, the poler also sticks to the shallowest safe water, and uses one of various techniques *(middle row)* to speed up, slow down, or even stop.

Going upstream or downstream, however, the poler tries always to keep the canoe directly aligned with the current —except for some brief moments during a maneuver called setting over, in which he carefully works the canoe across the current *(bottom row, far right)*. Otherwise, the force of moving water against the side of the tapered bow or stern may swivel the canoe violently off course, thus inviting it to broach to and upset.

Poling upstream on the starboard side, the canoeist grasps the pole near the center, left hand uppermost. He drops the pole's butt into the water just behind his right foot, applying light rearward pressure when the pole hits bottom (1). As the canoe moves forward, he reaches his right hand over the left (2), and continues with a hand-over-hand movement (3) known as climbing the pole. He then places a hand around or over the top of the pole (4), and gives a strong push. Finally, he flips the end of the pole smartly upward and out of the water (5), and slides his hands back for the next stroke.

Going downstream with a current (arrow), the canoeist controls his speed with a poling technique called snubbing. He grips the pole near the top with his hands about 18 inches apart. He then reaches forward at an angle of some 60° or more, depending on the current's strength and the water depths. Keeping the pole as close to the gunwale as possible, he probes the bottom for a good purchase (1). As the pole strikes bottom, he leans into it, crouching down slightly to keep his balance; the canoe will quickly decelerate. The canoeist retracts the pole from the water (2), and keeping his hands in the same position, he repeats the snubbing motion on the other side (3).

Three additional methods for controlling a canoe are illustrated at left. To hold the canoe in one spot when going downstream (far left), the canoeist thrusts the pole ahead of him, as when snubbing, but exerts continued pressure to bring the craft to a halt. To slow down, but not stop, some polers heading down sandy or muddy river beds drag the pole aft (center), pressing it down against the bottom.
To set over, or change course (near left), the canoeist poles his boat sideways across the current, pushing to the right when he wants to go left, as here, and thrusting to the left for a crabwise movement to the right. To compensate for the current's force, he thrusts ahead when going downstream and to the rear going upstream, and holds hard in either case so that the current will help carry the canoe over.

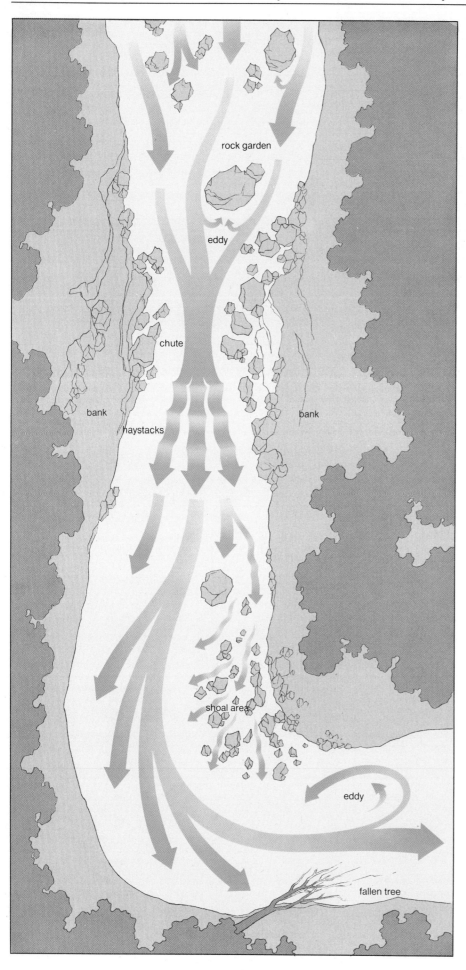

rock garden

eddy

chute

bank

haystacks

bank

shoal area

eddy

fallen tree

How to Run a River

The art of guiding a canoe down a swift-flowing river depends in part on the canoeist's ability to read water. On a stream like the one diagramed at left (and analyzed by segments in subsequent drawings), he must choose the safest channel by quick and continuing analysis of the various currents (blue arrows) that surge and eddy among obstacles along the stream's course. The other requirement for safe passage is the agile, muscular —and perfectly timed—paddling of the bowman and sternman.

When approaching a stretch of white water, both paddlers slide forward from their seats to kneel on the floor of the boat, thus lowering their weight and stabilizing the craft. As a general principle, they should stay parallel with the current —except when the main flow leads to a potential hazard, like the partially submerged tree in the river at left.

Steering decisions are handled by the person in the bow, who has a better view of what lies ahead. The bow paddler generally follows the V-shaped patches of unbroken water that signal a channel between partially submerged rocks. He initiates each turn with one or more of the special steering strokes—the draw, pry or sweep—shown on pages 96-97. And he shouts commands to the person in the stern, who strokes to align his end of the canoe with any change in direction.

The best way to maneuver through a set of obstacles may be by steady back-paddling, giving the canoeists extra seconds to align their craft in mid-current. Or, depending on the river's degree of difficulty (box, opposite), the safest course may be by land. If the bowman can see no clear passage through a tough stretch of white water, the canoeists should bring the craft ashore and reconnoiter from the bank. If still in doubt, they should portage to a point safely below the rapids.

This typical wilderness river, with its major currents represented by thick arrows and its offshoot currents by smaller ones, presents a challenging obstacle course for canoeists. Sets of mid-channel boulders, called rock gardens, churn the river into white-water rapids. Steep drops between narrow banks create fast-moving chutes. At the downstream end of a chute the water may pile up into large, standing wave crests called haystacks. At bends in the river, the current undermines the outside bank, causing underbrush and trees to pitch into the water, where they can easily ensnare a passing canoe.

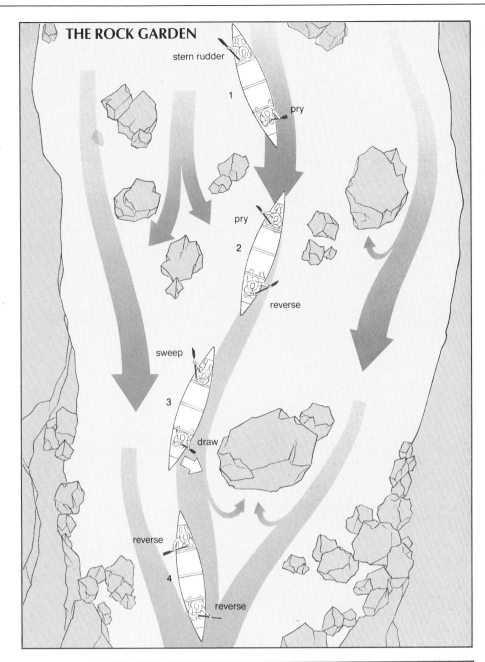

THE ROCK GARDEN

Approaching the rock garden the canoeists head for the main channel, the bowman making a tight turn to starboard with a sharp pry stroke while the aft paddler guides the stern around with a stern rudder (1). Repositioning the boat to negotiate the large boulder just downstream, the bowman continues to execute pry strokes (2) while the sternman back-paddles. As the bow clears the boulder, the bowman takes a few draw strokes while the sternman sweeps (3) to pivot the craft (white arrow) around the rock. Back in smooth water, both canoeists back-paddle (4) to prepare for the chute (overleaf).

A Paddler's Guide to White Water

White-water canoeists rate rivers by the severity of midstream hazards. Unobstructed streams flowing at less than four miles an hour are considered smooth water. Faster-flowing rivers are rated by the degrees of difficulty listed below.

I Easy: Sandy banks and bottom; no sharp bends; small riffles with regular, low waves.

II Medium: Frequent, unobstructed rapids; easy bends; regular waves; wide passages.

III Difficult: Numerous rapids with rocks; midstream eddies; narrow passages.

IV Very Difficult: Long stretches of rapids; irregular waves; large rocks; and abrupt bends. Mandatory reconnoitering before running. Precision maneuvering required.

V Extremely Difficult: Long, rocky rapids; steep gradient; big drops; hazardous eddies and crosscurrents. Only for experienced canoeists in watertight boats.

VI Limit of Navigability: Continuous violent rapids. Should be attempted only at favorable water levels and even then only by experts.

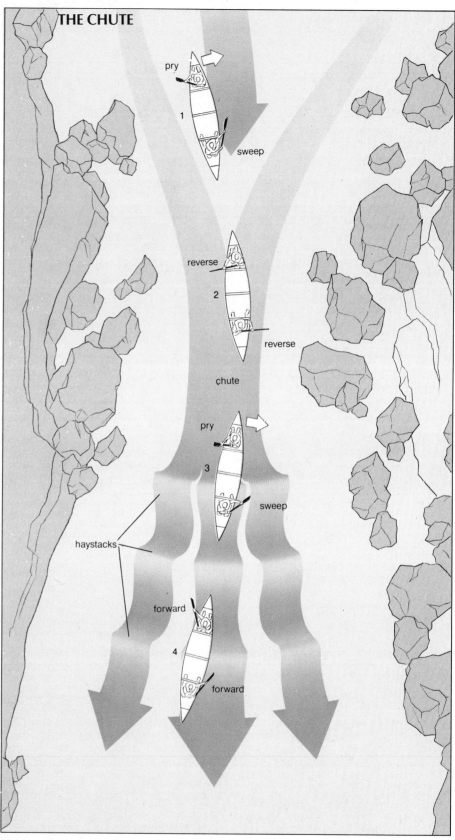

THE CHUTE

Nearing a chute, the paddlers combine sweep strokes in the bow and pry strokes astern to turn (white arrow) the canoe parallel with the main current (1). At the top of the chute, the canoeists back-paddle to slow their momentum (2) as they prepare to hit the cresting haystack waves directly downstream. To avoid cutting directly through the haystacks, and thus shipping water, the paddlers angle the canoe slightly to starboard (white arrow) with a combination of sweep and pry strokes (3). The craft then rides up and over the waves. Safely past the waves, the paddlers resume forward stroking (4).

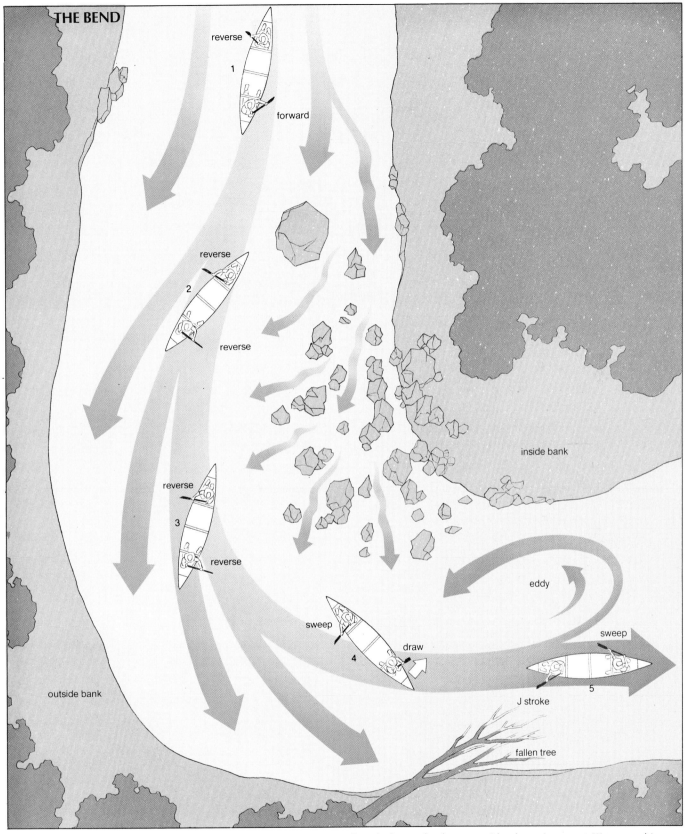

THE BEND

reverse
forward
1

reverse
2
reverse

reverse
3
reverse

sweep
4
draw

eddy
sweep
5
J stroke

fallen tree

inside bank

outside bank

Past the haystacks, the canoe rides the main current (1) approaching
a tight bend. Swept toward the outside bank, the paddlers begin
reversing (2) to check their speed so that they will stay near the inside
of the bend. By steady back-paddling (3), they avoid being swept
toward the fallen tree. The bow paddler takes a few rapid draw strokes
to clear the outer branches (white arrow), while the stern paddler
swings his end around with sweep strokes (4). Finally, the bow paddler
maneuvers away from the back eddy to port with a few sweep
strokes while the stern man helps with a J stroke.

At the start of their brief canoe trip on the Rio Grande, two paddlers stow provisions in their craft on the riverbank. Food, a camping tent and spare clothing are packed into separate watertight plastic bags, and then bundled into large canvas duffel bags to simplify loading and unloading. The bulk of the gear is packed under the center thwart to keep the canoe trimmed evenly fore and aft.

As one camper holds the bow line to guide the canoe after it is afloat, the two paddlers lower the fully packed craft down a steep bank into the river. The calm waters at this spot, a side channel downstream from a large island, make it an ideal launching place.

Payoff for Canoeists

After mastering basic strokes and steering techniques on a quiet lake or pond, the novice canoeist is ready to test himself on a short river trip, like the overnight expedition shown here on the Rio Grande. During this brief adventure, which took a party of 11 through the canyonlands of Big Bend National Park, the paddlers ran numerous rapids that dot the 40-mile stretch of river and portaged around a quarter-mile-long rock obstruction.

Before any paddling took place, however, the group plotted the route on paper, and designated as leader a veteran canoeist who had previously traversed the section they planned to cover. Wisely, they also planned to assemble at the launch site on the afternoon before the trip was to begin. There they sorted and organized their gear, and drove a car downriver to the take-out point so that canoes and paddlers could be ferried back to their parked cars at the end of the trip.

Early the next day, camping gear and provisions were packed into waterproof bags and evenly distributed in all five canoes (above, left). Once the canoes were launched, the group made its way downstream in single file, following the course set by the lead canoe and keeping a good 15 yards between boats to avoid pile-ups. Ironically, the lead canoe was harmlessly swamped (overleaf) by an unexpected crosscurrent. Except for this routine mishap the group completed the two-day voyage with no problems—and a major dividend of boat-handling experience and satisfaction.

A single file of canoes enters the narrow Santa Elena Canyon in the heart of Big Bend National Park. While traversing the 17-mile-long gorge—which has frequent shallow rapids, swift drops and tricky side currents—the canoeists wear their life jackets and allow plenty of room between boats to prevent any accidental piling up.

More than a mile into the Santa Elena Canyon two canoeists with a young passenger aboard stroke hard to prevent a strong crosscurrent from sweeping their craft toward a rocky wall at a sharp bend in the Rio Grande.

Just after turning over in some rapids, two drenched voyagers wade ashore in a stretch of calm water (above), carefully hanging onto their paddles and any loose gear that might otherwise float away. With the canoe safely ashore (right), they unloaded their waterproof bags and sleeping pads on the beach in order to bail out the water. Once the canoe was dry they repacked it and resumed paddling.

Four paddlers step out of their canoes to drag them through a shallow spot. Without their human cargo the canoes gain an inch or two of buoyancy, making it possible to tow them over the rocks rather than going through the long process of unloading and portaging.

At the end of the journey, after unloading all of their gear, the canyon runners lift their empty canoes over their heads and carry them from the riverbank to the roadhead.

THE CHALLENGE OF THE WILD RIVERS

Each spring and summer in the hills of the West and Northeast, snowmelt and rain surge into rocky river beds, making them navigable—but barely—for venturesome boatmen lured by the excitement of white water. In a strange assortment of custom-built and generally watertight craft of all shapes and sizes, warm-blooded sportsmen traverse icy rapids that would smash conventional wooden boats or swamp a canoe in a matter of seconds.

The biggest of these boats are inflatable 20-passenger pontoon rafts and rugged five-person rowing dories *(pages 116-119)*, which annually carry more than 36,000 adventurers down the Colorado River and other wilderness rivers such as Oregon's Rogue and Idaho's Salmon. But the predominant boat on streams like these is the one-man kayak, which is a lineal descendant of light, maneuverable sealskin-covered boats used by Eskimos. New hull materials, like fiberglass and rubberized canvas, make kayaks strong, yet flexible enough to bounce off jagged rocks without tearing or cracking.

Kayak handling, like construction, has progressed since the days of skin-covered boats. Paddlers are able to negotiate foaming stretches of rivers with a whole repertoire of sophisticated turning strokes developed to supplement classic techniques—like the Eskimo roll *(pages 112-113)*, which enables a kayaker to right himself from a total capsize in midstream.

So skilled have kayakers become in the past two decades that they have gone beyond the challenge of simply negotiating rapids to develop a whole new sport called slalom racing, in which contestants struggle through a tight midstream obstacle course *(pages 114-115)*. Today slalom races are staged on scores of mountain rivers from Maine to California. And in 1972 kayak slalom racing received the sportsman's ultimate form of acceptance: it was made an Olympic sport.

Two kayakers zigzag around a submerged ledge in Colorado's upper
Arkansas River. Most challenging in early June at the height of
the spring runoff, the river cascades through a valley near the Sawatch
Range of the Colorado Rockies. The frothing chute shown here is
part of a particularly favored stretch of the river, which features five
major rapids and a drop of some 400 feet in just over six miles.

A well-equipped kayaker plunges downstream through a cresting wave on the Kanderoseros River in upstate New York. He controls the boat with short, quick strokes of a double-bladed paddle, using a circular arm motion roughly similar to the leg action required to pedal a bicycle. The yellow nylon spray skirt attached by a quick-release mechanism to the cockpit's rim makes the craft fully watertight. His other white-water equipment includes a flotation jacket for buoyancy, a neoprene wet suit with insulated gloves to provide for warmth in icy water and a plastic safety helmet.

A Skintight Craft

Just as the centaur of mythology was part man and part horse, the kayak paddler is part man, part boat. More than any other mariner, the kayaker must learn—through hours of instruction and weeks of practice—to make his fragile, tippy craft an extension of his body, a floating limb capable of responding to the split-second moves on which even his life may depend.

Fortunately, the spindle-shaped vessel is ideally equipped to meet the challenge. A recreational kayak floats like a leaf, drawing only two to three inches of water when fully loaded, and it answers instantly to the lightest touch of the double-bladed paddle. The paddler, seated in a cockpit in the middle of the boat with his legs stretched out under the deck toward the bow, literally wears the boat like a garment on his lower body. Interior supports for the hips, knees and feet steady him and provide the hull contact essential for a special set of strokes called braces, which work through a combination of paddle handling and upper-body English.

Through proper use of these strokes, the kayaker can turn the craft on a dime, upstream or down, at high speeds in rough water. This maneuverability is vital for dodging obstructions, which can do lethal damage. Though kayaks are tougher than their graceful appearance would suggest, their fiberglass hulls can snap like a twig when pinned by a 10-mile-an-hour current against a midstream boulder or a bridge abutment. And a kayaker flung from his boat into an icy mountain stream by such a mishap can quickly lose consciousness and drown or succumb to exposure, if not properly equipped with a helmet, life jacket and wet suit.

Bracing strokes, which demand quick shifts of balance, are best mastered by instruction in a swimming pool or on other calm water. And no one should venture into white water without having learned a maneuver called the Eskimo roll. This is a combination stroke and body twist that will return a paddler to an upright position after a partial tip-over or even a total capsize in rapids, as shown on pages 112-113.

Like all expert paddlers, the kayaker makes the river work for him. He uses so-called pillows of water that build upstream from partly submerged rocks to help steer the boat around such treacherous obstacles. And like the man in the lower picture on the opposite page, the kayak paddler exploits the eddies created by big rocks or sharp curves in a channel as convenient parking places in which to enjoy a short breather.

A kayaker braces for a turn in boiling white water. By leaning to the right while holding his right-hand blade in the water, with the blade at a 45° angle to the bow, he inclines the boat to the right. In this position, with the paddle acting as a pivot, the force of the current will turn the boat as much as 180°.

Resting in a large eddy, a kayaker soaks up some early spring sunshine before continuing down Vermont's Black River. The main current swirls to the left of the snow-blanketed rock, leaving a pool where the boat can remain stationary indefinitely.

In this sequence, a kayaker paddling against a tidal current in an inlet on the Maine coast recovers from an accidental capsize by executing an Eskimo roll, the maneuver diagramed on the opposite page. Here the bow of the kayak sinks into the trough of a large wave. In another instant, the boat will pitchpole forward, submerging the kayaker beneath his overturned craft (below).

Completely capsized, and submerged save only for his gloves and paddle, the kayaker is calmly going into the key phase of his Eskimo roll. Hanging head down under his boat, he extends his paddle to the surface of the water —as shown in drawing No. 2 opposite—in preparation for swinging himself upright.

With a heave on the paddle and a twist of his upper torso, the kayaker comes up out of the water. In a series of moves lasting less than three seconds he has managed to right himself and regain control of his craft.

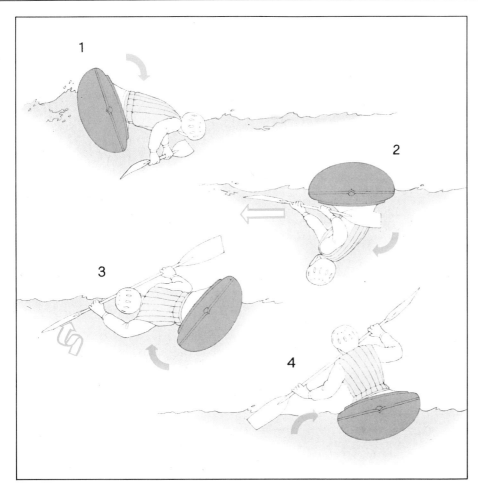

As a capsized kayaker feels his boat being tipped over to starboard (1), he begins an Eskimo roll by leaning toward the bow, keeping his head down and the shaft of his paddle approximately parallel to the starboard gunwale. Once upside down (2), he extends the left-hand blade out from the boat (white arrow) and near the surface, so that the shaft is at an angle of about 30° to the boat. He then thrusts his body upward (3), while rapidly sculling the left-hand blade back and forth (wavy arrow). This combination of movements snaps the boat upright (4) to complete the roll.

Popping a Souse Hole

Expert kayakers often toy with the swirling currents in a white-water river for sheer fun. The paddler above, apparently pitchpoling over, is actually about to pop a souse hole, a hot-dog maneuver that will bounce him downstream. Souse holes form when water pouring over the downstream side of a barely submerged rock scoops a depression in the river bed and creates a dip in the surface of the river. As the paddler noses his kayak upstream, the bow drops into the hole until the current catches the boat and pops it back. The force of water in a big souse hole can propel a kayak end over end up to 20 feet.

White-Water Slalom

The apex of white-water running is slalom competition, in which every stroke and maneuver in kayaking and canoeing are called into play. In a typical slalom race, contestants in solo kayaks or in one- or two-person decked-over canoes traverse a twisting route like the one shown here, which combines natural hazards, such as rocks and rapids, with a maze of man-made difficulties.

A slalom course can be up to 800 meters long, winding through a series of so-called gates the racers must go through. These gates are pairs of striped poles hung 4 to 11 feet apart from cables above the course. To negotiate the course successfully the racer needs a tightrope walker's sense of balance and the muscle to handle his strokes against the weight of thundering water. For example, at a reverse gate he must stop in midcareer, turn his boat end for end and go through the gate stern first, then swing around and head downstream again. At other gates he must make a complete circle, approaching them from downstream and then paddling through against the current.

Contestants who brush a gate pole—or miss a gate entirely—incur penalties in the form of seconds tacked on to their elapsed times. And if a racer capsizes while passing through a gate, 50 seconds are added to his time—enough to put him permanently out of the running.

A typical slalom course includes up to 18 color-coded gates spaced out over a half mile of river. Three kinds of gates challenge the paddler's skills and reflexes. Forward gates, the most numerous on any course, have green poles to starboard, facing downstream. Even more demanding are the two types of gates with reversed poles. Upstream gates, such as numbers 4, 9, 10 and 15, are usually set in eddies and backwaters, and require 360° turns to traverse. Reverse gates, such as numbers 5R, 11R and 13R, must be entered backward.

start
finish

Making a turn out of an upstream slalom gate during an Eastern United States Championship Race on Vermont's West River, a kayaker leans out to execute a bracing stroke that will pivot him back into the main current—which is flowing from left to right.

Two kayakers thrash down a giant slalom course on the roiling Isère River in southeastern France. From the starting pennant upstream, the racers have paddled their boats one at a time through a series of gates that dangle from overhead wires. The upstream paddler has just brushed the green pole of gate 8, a mistake that will add 10 penalty seconds to his score. At gate 12, which is marked with the letter R to show that it is a reverse gate, the other contestant struggles to turn his craft so that he can run through the gate with the stern first.

Nearly a mile below the Grand Canyon's rim, an oarsman and four passengers drift on a glassy stretch of the Colorado. Though the surface here—as in much of the river—is unbroken by rocks, the current sucks the dory along at three to four knots; even while resting, an oarsman must watch for riffles indicating underwater obstructions.

Masters of the Canyon

The most awesome stretch of boatable white water in America thunders through 277 miles of the Grand Canyon of the Colorado River. In its course, it descends 2,000 feet in the roar of some 96 rapids at speeds that occasionally exceed 19 miles per hour. During the months of May through September, when the Colorado is at its fullest, some 12,000 riders go booming through this marine roller coaster. Most of them run the river in flexible rubber rafts; but for real white-water purists, the way to go is in a wooden dory like those shown on these pages.

These river dories are direct descendants of craft designed more than a century ago to carry fishermen and trappers down such wild rivers as Oregon's McKenzie and California's Klamath.

Roughly 18 feet long, 7 to 8 feet in the beam, flat-bottomed and nearly double-ended, river dories can carry four passengers and an experienced professional oarsman-skipper. With this load, plus food and camping gear for a three-week outing, the dories draw less than a foot of water. Because of watertight storage lockers, fore and aft, they stay afloat even when swamped. And the marine plywood construction (stronger and lighter than the double-lapped oak of the original boats) makes them so sturdy that they can survive anything short of a full-tilt, head-on collision with a boulder. Even then, the oarsman can usually seal small leaks with a caulking compound that hardens to a metal-like finish, and have his boat floating again in a few hours. Should one or both of the 10-foot-long ash oars break, a spare pair is carried, lashed to the deck.

These dories were not introduced to the Colorado until 1962. But they proved so riverworthy that passengers now pay as much as $250 per week for the ride of their lives through great walls of spray, deep roiling holes and curling breakers. Even though the hazards of the river have claimed two lives in the last 14 years from riders in other kinds of craft, no one has perished or been injured in a dory skippered by a professional river hand.

Approaching a patch of white water, the oarsman steers around a submerged rock, being careful to stay in the green tongue of smooth dark water that indicates a safe channel. Once the 12-knot current has sucked him past the rocks, he will stroke on his port oar to pivot the dory into mid-current to take the next series of waves head on.

Oarsman and passengers brace for a drenching as their dory plunges toward a 15-foot standing wave. The wave, formed by the rush of water over a sudden drop, curls like an ocean comber and breaks upriver in a constant mass of white foam. Dories crash head on through these waves with surprising ease, and the desert air of the Grand Canyon's floor quickly dries both passengers and cargo.

Passengers grip the gunwales as a dory rears against a cresting wall of water during a wild, 20-mph ride through a rapid called Granite Falls. In heavy white water like this, the oarsman, who faces downstream, must keep the boat's bow always pointing into the waves to prevent broaching and capsizing. All hands wear life jackets in case he makes a mistake.

THE SIMPLE LIFE A LA MODE

The fashionable cure for urban ennui in the latter part of the 19th Century—as it would be a century later—was a return to nature. Each summer, waves of affluent New Yorkers set out for the rivers and lakes of Maine, the marshlands of the Jersey shore, and the mountains of upstate New York, where they settled into elaborately rustic lodges. There, clad in stylish tweeds, or summer skirts and blouses, they absorbed the revivifying beauty of the woods and streams—without the inconvenience of actually roughing it.

By far the most stylish retreat was the lake country in the New York Adirondack Mountains, a region of timbered uplands that offered some of the most bracing air, restoring vistas, and lively fishing and hunting in the country. Accommodations were emphatically posh. One of the most popular hostelries was Martin's, on Lower Saranac Lake. There, one visitor from New York City reported, "You have a fair bed, an excellent table, with trout and venison *ad libitum,* and can loiter and fish and hunt in the vicinity."

The main attraction, of course, was the lakes themselves and their connecting streams, which were not only filled with trout but provided an effortless way to get around. The same chronicler noted that you could "go through lakes dotted with islands, through ponds, along rivers, and not be compelled to walk altogether farther than from City Hall to Union Square."

The conveyance that allowed the tourist to explore the countryside without using his feet was a marvelous craft called the Adirondack guide boat, which com-

bined the lightness of a canoe with the roominess and stability of a New England dory. The outdoorsman from the city—called a "sport" in the local vernacular—would lounge against a back rest, while a guide rowed him to the prime picnic grounds, fishing holes and deer runs.

It was not New Yorkers alone who flocked to the area. On any given holiday, some of the world's most powerful and celebrated people of the Victorian era could be found taking their ease in the Adirondacks. President Grover Cleveland arrived in the summer of 1884 for a three-week stay. Victoria's own maid of honor breezed in at age 60, carrying a case of plum pudding and a special "portable soup" from London.

Even Ralph Waldo Emerson vacationed here, and was ferried by guide boat to his first deer hunt. According to a member of his party, at first Emerson "declined to take any part in the hunting or fishing, but we had not long been in camp before he caught the temper of the occasion....He said to me one day: 'I must kill a deer before we go home, even if the guide has to hold him by the tail.'" Fortunately for his later reputation as a preservationist, mighty hunter Emerson never did get his trophy. But he did not hold that against the guides who led the hunt; he memorialized them in the poem "The Adirondacks": "Look to yourselves, ye polished gentlemen! No city airs or arts pass current here. Your rank is all reversed; let men of cloth bow to the stalwart churls in overalls: *They* are the doctors of the wilderness, And we the low-prized laymen."

A guide gently maneuvers his craft into the hummocky marshland at the head of an Adirondack lake while a sport in the stern helps steer with a paddle. "To glide along, while the waves ripple up against the sides with a softly murmuring cadence, illustrates the very poetry of motion," rhapsodized one early visitor to the area, who likened his Adirondack sojourn to "the enchanted life of the lotus-eater."

A party of four guides and their sports prepares to embark upon an outing in Lower Saranac Lake in 1876. Their double-ended guide boats—beamy, stable and lightweight —represented a handy compromise between a dory and a canoe, making them perfect craft for lake travel. The boats could be safely rowed across open water, or paddled down narrow streams and through rapids.

With his boat hoisted aloft, a guide approaches the placid shore of Blue Mountain Lake, as his sport totes the oars. Made of thin strips of pine over ribs cut from spruce roots, guide boats weighed only 60 to 80 pounds and were easy to shoulder during a carry—the Adirondack term for portage. Yet the craft were sturdy enough to float three men and their provisions.

A nattily turned-out hunting party—the men in tweeds and boots, the ladies in taffeta skirts—starts out along Sweeny Carry from Upper Saranac Lake to the Raquette River, three miles down the road. The building at left is the 75-room Wawbeek Lodge, which supplied the buckboards that were used for hauling the guide boats at $1.50 per vessel.

At the guide house for the Paul Smith Hotel on the lower St. Regis Lake, one old Adirondack hand caulks his craft's stern with white lead while another inspects his boat's bottom. Each guide owned his vessel, and would wait for customers at a boathouse like this, kept by one of the big hotels. Among the regulars to whom Paul Smith guides hired out were Grover Cleveland and P. T. Barnum.

A vacationer takes a solo early-morning row offshore from the imposing Prospect House on Blue Mountain Lake. When Prospect House opened for business in 1882, it was considered the last word in backwoods posh, with five rambling stories, which were served by steam-powered elevators. Better yet, it was the very first hotel in the world to have electric lights in every room.

A guide running the rapids of an Adirondack stream steers from the stern with a paddle, while the sport in the bow warns of upcoming obstructions. To slip safely through stretches of quick water, the guide boats required close coordination between all hands. At such times, one traveler warned, "You should have your hair parted strictly in the middle."

Nine decorous members of the Horican Sketching Club, garbed in ankle-length skirts and sunbonnets, render their versions of the view from an island in Lake George. Besides sketching, Adirondack ladies botanized in the woods, played charades at night, and wrote it all down in copious letters and diaries.

Eighty-four-year-old Alvah Dunning, retired patriarch of Adirondack guides, dozes over a pair of fly rods near the shore of Sagamore Lake in 1899. The sublime ease of such moments, pleasantly interrupted by the strike of a speckled trout, was precisely what pulled weary city folk to the lake country.

A hunter and his guide head back to camp, triumphantly bearing a 10-point buck taken during a day of deerstalking along Upper Saranac Lake. Considered at the time to be the ultimate in genteel backwoodsmanship, deerstalking by guide boat virtually guaranteed a trophy. A pair of hounds would flush a deer from the woods, forcing it into the water, where it became a clear mark for anyone with a rifle. So easy were the kills, in fact, that in 1897 New York State judged this form of deer hunting to be unsportsman-like, and banned it.

4 Back in 1922, 18-year-old Ralph Samuelson strapped a pair of eight-foot-long steam-molded pine boards onto his feet, grasped a tape-wrapped metal ring that was tied to a motorboat by a 100-foot length of sash cord and took off across Minnesota's Lake Pepin on what is generally acknowledged to be the world's first successful water-skiing run. His towboat was a 24-foot inboard launch equipped with a six-cylinder, 24-horsepower gasoline engine capable of poking along at a top speed of 16 miles per hour—which is just about the practical minimum for keeping a skier up on his skis and planing. Today, Samuelson's epic feat is routinely emulated by some 12 million enthusiastic Amer-

THE CATALYST IN WATER-SKIING

icans, like the man at left, who have mastered the art of skimming along the surface of the water. And the boats that pull these skiers have proliferated and changed dramatically.

The modern water-skier rides behind one of an array of quick, light, high-powered craft that are capable of reaching speeds of up to 35 miles per hour in a matter of only seconds. It has been the development of such fast and relatively inexpensive towboats that has made skiing second only to fishing in popularity among water sports. In fact, market surveys over the last 30 years have shown that more than 40 per cent of American outboard-boat purchasers list water-skiing as a major reason for buying their craft.

But though a fast boat and a willing skier are the basic ingredients of water-skiing, the catalyst that makes them work well together is the boat driver. There is much more involved in his task than the deceptively simple routine of accelerating quickly and smoothly to get the skier up on the surface, and then speeding along at a fast, steady clip to keep him there. Any normally competent boat handler can manage that part of it. However, a good towboat driver is most often a knowledgeable and competent water-skier himself. Thus he will know from his own experience and his gut instinct how to shove the throttle to the position that will produce the fastest acceleration and the safest planing speed for a given skier, based on the skier's size, skill and confidence. The boat driver must be prepared to respond immediately to a skier's hand signals calling for changes in boat speed or direction, and he must also be ready to come about swiftly when a skier falls, in order to return the towline or to pick up the skier.

The operator of the boat must accomplish all this while observing the safety rules and local boating regulations, which sometimes restrict speeds—or even prohibit skiing—in certain areas. Even more important for the good towboat driver is the ability to resist what is often a strong temptation to show off his boat's speed and maneuverability. This is usually done at the expense of the skier, who may be dunked or even injured.

An even greater degree of precise and tightly disciplined boat handling is required of drivers who tow competitors in local, regional and national tournaments. For the majority of tournaments, drivers are divided into three classes—assistant, regular and senior—and only the best are invited to drive in major competitions like the National Water Ski Championships. Drivers in the championships must be senior class, and only six are chosen each year from around the country. A driver is assigned an entire event that may require more than four hours of continuous activity. In the slaloms, the driver must make critical adjustments in speed and steering to compensate for the varying strengths and styles of as many as 60 to 70 different skiers while running a 285-yard course to within two tenths of a second of the prescribed time. His performance must be at the virtuoso level, rivaling that of the champion skier. For if it is not, the skier simply will not be the champion.

As a summer sunset gilds the rumpled waters of the Ohio River near East Liverpool, Ohio, a water-skier heads for home inside the wake of his outboard-powered towboat.

Equipping a Towboat

The basic requirement for a water-skiing towboat is the ability to accelerate quickly and smoothly to a speed of at least 20 miles per hour with a skier in tow. This requirement is so easy to meet that dozens of craft from small outboard utility boats to high-powered inboards qualify. But for the more than a million boatowners who use their vessels primarily or exclusively for skiing, the proper craft must meet far more demanding specifications.

A good towboat, like the 16-foot modified stock runabout at right, is relatively light, highly maneuverable and generously powered. Its light-displacement hull has a V-shaped bow tapering to an almost flat stern for easy planing—an important consideration, since a boat up on a plane throws off almost no wake to unbalance the skier. Its power plant can be either inboard, stern drive or outboard, so long as it delivers enough horsepower to push it steadily along at competition speeds of 36 miles per hour.

Another requirement for the hull is that it should be fairly wide abeam—from 60 to 70 inches on a 16-footer like the one shown. The beaminess keeps the boat stable on turns—and, along with an uncluttered cockpit, provides storage space for skis, flotation vests and towlines *(page 132)*. Another key feature is low freeboard, which improves the driver's side vision and makes it easy for skiers to climb in and out. The helm should be set well forward for clear visibility ahead; for this reason all towboats, including outboards, should be equipped with a wheel.

In modifying a stock boat for towing, the most important step is to secure a towline hitch in such a way as to give the skier maximum freedom of movement while preventing the line from coming in contact with the motor. The simple transom hitch *(center opposite)* is well suited for most recreational skiing. But it can create steering problems for slalom skiing, where the heavy lateral pull exerted by a skier tends to jerk the stern from side to side. On a well-outfitted boat, this problem is overcome by means of a sturdy metal pylon like the one rigged to the boat at top, with a center post secured near where the boat pivots on high-speed turns.

Because of the importance of maintaining signal communications with the skier *(page 133)*, a properly equipped towboat includes a large rearview mirror for the driver and a rear-facing seat for an observer who constantly monitors the skier, watches out for spills and conveys instructions from skier to skipper.

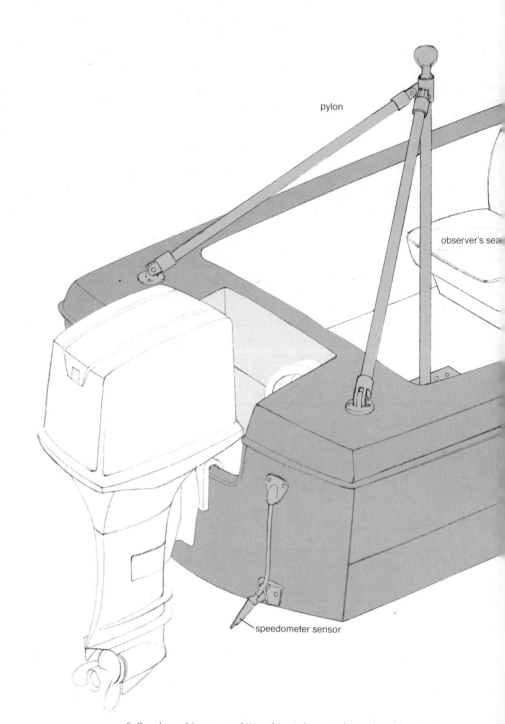

pylon

observer's sea[t]

speedometer sensor

Fully adapted for water-skiing, this 16-foot stock runabout has a 75-horsepower outboard motor for fast acceleration to a comfortable skiing speed of 20 to 25 miles per hour. The towrope is hitched to a pylon of steel tubing with a center post locked into a metal plate on the deck and braced by two legs attached to the transom. The steering console includes a tachometer and a speedometer, which has an especially accurate sensing device on the transom. A rearview mirror enables the driver to keep an eye on the skier and anticipate directions from the observer in the rear-facing seat. A ladder, shipped when the boat is underway, helps the skier over the side.

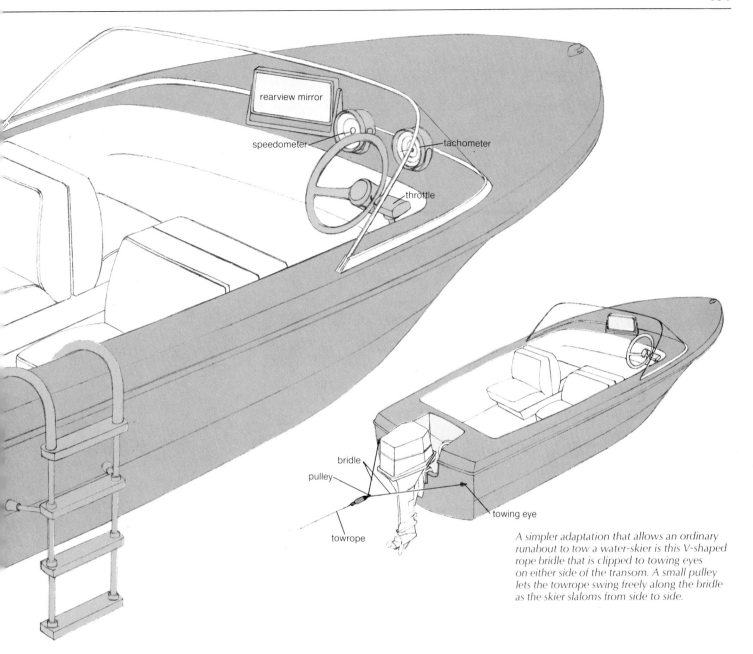

A simpler adaptation that allows an ordinary runabout to tow a water-skier is this V-shaped rope bridle that is clipped to towing eyes on either side of the transom. A small pulley lets the towrope swing freely along the bridle as the skier slaloms from side to side.

A Skier's Superboat

Built specially for water-skiing from its semi-V hull up, this 18-foot competition ski boat is a high-performance craft like those used in major tournaments. A 250-horsepower inboard engine can propel the one-ton boat smoothly at 36 miles per hour, even with driver and observer aboard and a hefty skier in tow. A seven-foot beam lends stability; fins set on the underside of the hull just fore and aft of the towing post, or pylon, also make the craft more stable. A key feature of the dashboard instrumentation—which also includes tachometer, ammeter, fuel gauge, water-temperature gauge and oil-pressure gauge—is a pair of speedometers. The extra one assures the driver of a backup reading should one of them fail.

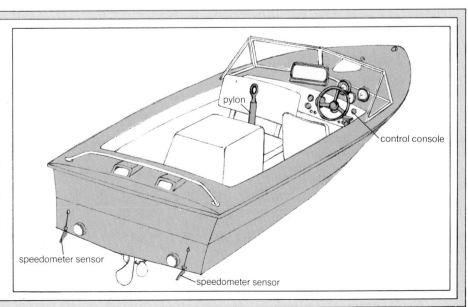

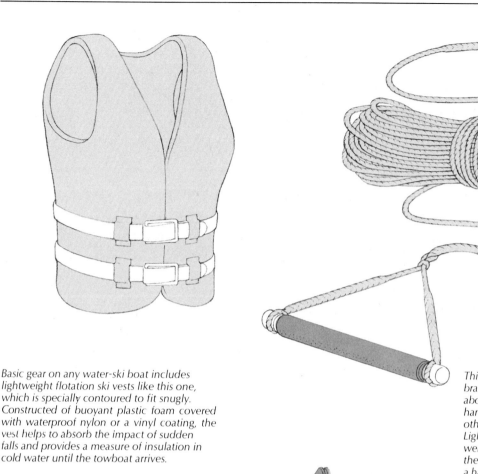

Basic gear on any water-ski boat includes lightweight flotation ski vests like this one, which is specially contoured to fit snugly. Constructed of buoyant plastic foam covered with waterproof nylon or a vinyl coating, the vest helps to absorb the impact of sudden falls and provides a measure of insulation in cold water until the towboat arrives.

This standard 75-foot towline of ¼-inch braided polypropylene, coiled for stowage aboard a boat, has a floating, foam-covered handle at one end and an eye splice at the other end for securing to the tow hitch. Lightweight and water resistant, the line weighs less than a pound and floats freely on the surface—and can withstand more than a half ton of pressure without snapping.

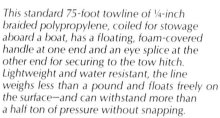

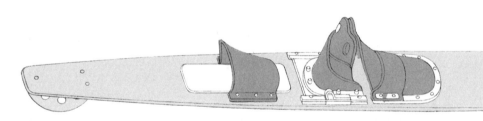

These four skis are for a progression of skiing skills. At top is a beginner's ski of wood or fiberglass, about 5½ feet long and 6 inches wide with a stabilizing keel; it has an adjustable heel piece for a close fit. The competition slalom ski below it has reinforced bindings to anchor the front foot, a second toe piece for the rear foot and a perforated fin for smooth direction changes. The short, lightweight trick ski has an angled rear binding for one-ski stunts. The jump ski at bottom has custom bindings mounted on metal for reinforcement on hard landings.

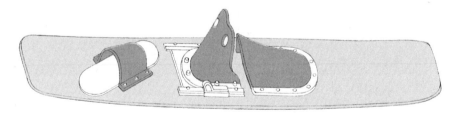

Signals the Ski Boatman Must Memorize

The principal method of communication that exists between a water-skier and his boat driver and observer is the set of distinctive hand signals below, developed by the American Water Ski Association. With only two exceptions, their meanings are self-explanatory. A whip-off signal means that the skier wants the boat to run closer to the shore, where he will cut sharply across the wake, turn parallel to the shoreline, then release the towrope and coast to a stop in shallow water. The clasped-hands signal indicates that a fallen skier is down but not injured.

1 SPEED UP

2 SLOW DOWN

3 SPEED OK

4 STOP

5 CUT MOTOR

6 TURN RIGHT

7 WHIP OFF

8 RETURN TO DOCK

9 FALLEN SKIER OK

Towing Techniques

A close partnership between the driver of a towboat and a water-skier begins from the moment the skier shouts "In gear!" to signal his readiness for the start of a run and lasts until the moment when he whips off at the end *(page 137)*. The skier may choose to begin the run with a standard in-water start, as shown in the sequence at near right, or he may opt for the more difficult but drier off-the-dock start *(opposite, top)*—a popular alternative when the water is cold. With either technique, it is up to the driver to bring the skier smoothly and quickly to his feet, by accelerating to the desired planing speed of 20 to 25 miles per hour as rapidly as possible without jerking the towrope.

Once underway, the driver selects a course in sheltered water that is relatively free of other boats, following any hand-signal instructions from the skier. To give the skier a long, smooth straightaway with a minimum number of turns, the driver may execute a compact bar-bell pattern *(opposite, bottom)*. But he should avoid abrupt directional changes—except when getting around such unexpected obstacles as floating planks or stray swimmers. Should the skier fall, the driver must be prepared to circle back immediately, and either to redeliver the towline to the ski-er, or to pick him up if he does not wish to continue *(page 136)*.

Often, the return to dock or beach front at the end of the run can be the most challenging part of the trip for both skier and driver, for it generally brings them into shallow, traffic-congested waters where a slight miscalculation can send the skier skidding off into a dock or other boats—or may cause him to hit the shoaling bottom and pitch forward onto his face.

For in-water starts, the observer hands the coiled towline to the skier, and the driver moves gradually away until the entire length of the towline has straightened out flat in the water. The driver then shifts into neutral, allowing the skier to get into position to start, with her ski-tips out of the water and the line running between them. When the skier shouts "In gear!" the driver idles forward to take up any remaining slack line (top). As soon as the line is taut, the skier shouts "Hit it!" and the driver accelerates straight ahead to pull the skier up (center) until she is planing along the surface (bottom).

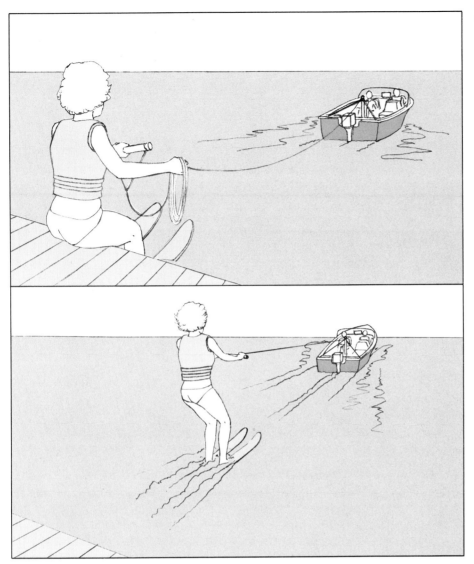

A take-off from the dock begins with the skier seated at the dock's edge, with the coiled towline in one hand and the handle in the other. At the "in gear" command, the driver idles forward (top), slowly drawing the coiled line from the skier's hand. When about 10 feet of line are left, the skier tosses the last few coils into the water and yells "Hit it!" The driver then moves forward at full throttle, pulling the skier off the dock directly into the planing position (bottom). When properly executed, the dock start is not only jolt-free, but requires less pulling effort from the boat than does the in-water start.

This towing pattern, only about 350 yards long, is often used to ski in crowded areas. The driver must maintain an even speed both on the straightaway and on the broad turns, which should be at least 80 yards in diameter; otherwise, the line will go slack. The turns are always executed in the same clockwise or counterclockwise direction, depending on the predominant traffic pattern in the area. As the boat completes each turn and begins a new straightaway run, the driver attempts to steer a course through the center of his own previous wake, thus allowing the skier to enjoy smooth water at all times.

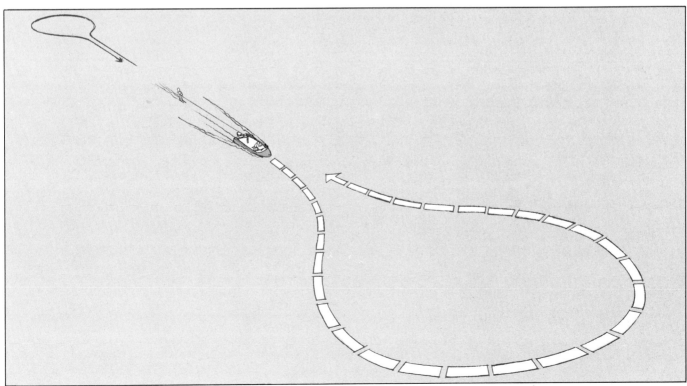

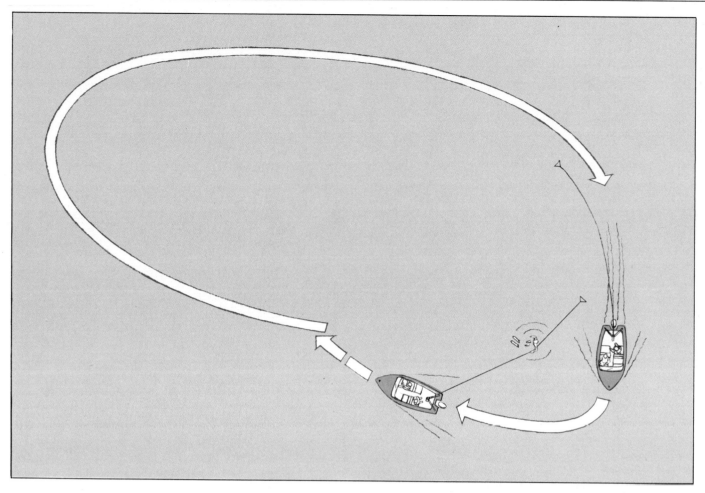

To return the towline to a fallen skier, the boat driver makes a circle, turning in a direction that keeps the skier continually in view—e.g., if the helm is on the boat's starboard side, as here, the driver turns clockwise. As he approaches the skier, the driver reduces speed to idle and steers for a point about 8 to 10 feet away from the skier. When he passes this point, he cuts in sharply. This maneuver draws the towline to the inside of the turn and directly toward the skier, who grasps the line loosely, letting it slip through her fingers until the handle comes to her. The driver then waits for the signal to begin another in-water start in the boat's original direction.

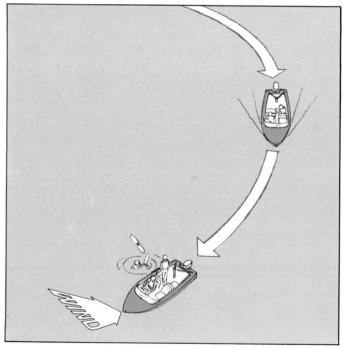

When picking up a weary skier, the driver circles back, making his approach from downwind. When he is about two to five boat lengths below the skier, depending on wind and current strength, he comes up into the wind and idles forward, keeping the skier on the same side as his helm location. For the last few feet, the motor is shifted to neutral. As the boat's momentum carries it abreast of the skier, the observer stands ready to help her up the boarding ladder.

To land a skier at a dock or on a beach, the boat driver should approach on a course parallel with the shore front and about 50 to 100 feet out, keeping a steady speed of about 20 miles per hour. As the boat nears the landing area, the skier pulls on the towline and turns toward land; the tug on the line and the centrifugal force of the turn will give her the momentum to coast in after she releases the towline. She then lets go of the handle and planes free (dotted arrow). If boatman and skier time everything properly, the free skier will slow down and sink a few feet from the landing point.

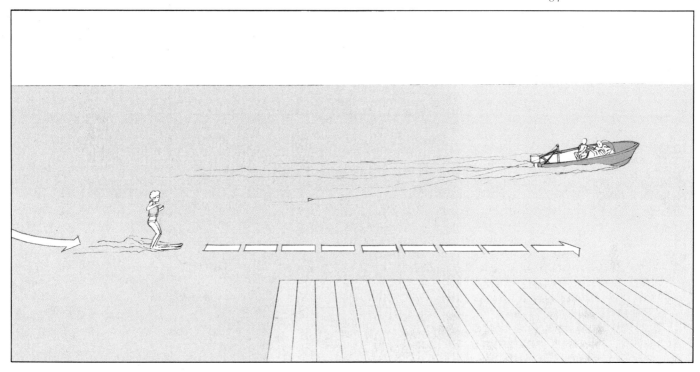

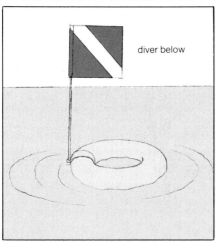

diver below

Safety Tips for Drivers

Ultimate responsibility for the safety of all participants in a water-skiing expedition rests firmly on the shoulders of the driver, who should follow scrupulously the safety rules listed below.

● Pick a course that is free of hazards, including boats, floats, rocks, piers and any debris floating in the water. Be especially watchful for swimmers and for warning flags like the one at left, indicating the presence of skin divers below the surface. Keep well clear of possible shoal areas close to shore.

● Carry as few passengers as possible in order to give maximum visibility to driver and observer, to avoid unnecessary distractions and to reduce weight for good engine performance. All passengers should be safely seated and never permitted to perch on the gunwales, bow or transom during a run.

● Insist that the skier wear a reliable flotation device.

● Never tailgate another towboat; its skier may fall directly into your path and be injured by your hull or propeller. If a boat tailgates you, signal your skier and move out of the way.

● Never turn the boat while the skier is cutting outside of your wake, as in slaloming. If he has cut to the inside of the turn, the towline will go slack and he will begin to sink. If he is outside the turn, he will be whipped around suddenly and may go out of control.

● Avoid skiing at night.

Advanced Skiing

Once a boat driver and a skier have acquired the skills and teamwork required for basic skiing, they are ready to try the more difficult and spectacular maneuvers of competitive and exhibition skiing. For the skier this means trading his pair of recreational skis for a single slalom ski, or the other specialized skis used for jumping and trick skiing. For the boat driver, it means more precise driving—and even greater attention to the relationship between boat and skier.

In competition slalom, the skipper repeatedly tows the skier at the end of a 75-foot rope over a course like the one partially diagramed at bottom. Typically he begins with a run of 30 miles per hour and moves the speed up to 36 miles per hour. Once the highest speed is reached, the towline is gradually shortened in succeeding runs until each skier but one—the winner—faults out. As the rope becomes shorter, centrifugal force on the turns will accelerate the skier to 70 miles per hour, and he will exert a pull on the towboat that is more than triple his own weight.

The other types of advanced skiing put their own kinds of special demands on the boat handler, from the precise approach that is vital for the ski jumper *(page 140),* to the carefully coordinated speed control that lifts a kite skier off the water *(pages 142-143)* and keeps him safely dangling 10 to 30 feet in the air.

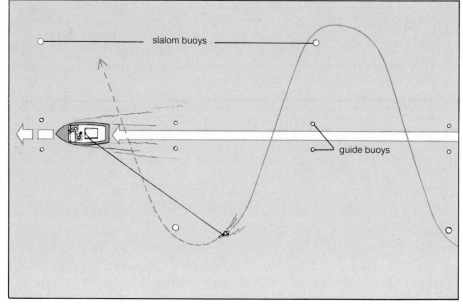

This segment of a regulation competition slalom course illustrates the contrasting paths taken by skier and towboat. The driver follows an arrow-straight, 285-yard course, maintaining a precise speed and shaving through a succession of guide buoys three yards wide and spaced at 45-yard intervals. The skier behind him traces a weaving pattern around a series of six slalom buoys set on alternate sides of the boat's path at a distance of 12½ yards from the course's center line.

On the tournament slalom course in San Diego's Mission Bay, a skier expertly cuts across the wake of his towboat toward the buoy at lower right. At the top level of competition the boat handler's job takes such skill and finesse that, for the U.S. national championships, only a few dozen of the most highly rated drivers from around the country qualify. Each driver may tow as many as 40 skiers in a single event, a task so demanding that one driver calls it the "toughest, coldest, hottest, most miserable job" on the water.

A tournament skier spews up a rooster's tail of spray as he accelerates out of a turn at a speed of more than 60 miles an hour, pulling against his towline with nearly 400 pounds of pressure. As he prepares to round the next buoy, his pull on the towline will decrease. A good driver must anticipate these regular changes in line tension, and continually make minor throttle and steering adjustments to keep the boat moving smoothly and evenly.

Jumping and Tricking

Streaking for the take-off ramp at close
to 60 miles per hour, a competition jumper
completes the second of two sharp turns,
which boost his speed to almost double that
of the boat. As the skier swings out and back,
the driver works both throttle and helm
to keep his own speed at a constant 35 miles
per hour and his course straight, as in the
diagram at right. When the skier zooms up
the ramp's waxed incline and into the air as
far as 180 feet, tension on the line will
suddenly decrease; the driver must be ready
to throttle down to maintain constant speed.

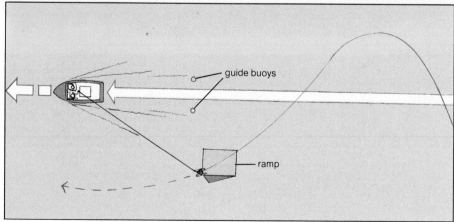

This spectacular jump somersault, performed at the end of a 50-foot line just after the driver has towed the skier over a jump ramp at 16 miles per hour, requires such split-second timing and coordination that the slightest variation in the towboat's course or a change in boat speed of one mile per hour could result in a fall—and inevitable sacrifice of points in a tournament. Most trick-skiing routines are performed within a speed range of 16 to 19 miles per hour; in each case the driver's boat handling must be near perfect and his speedometer pin-point accurate to carry the skier through.

Kiting

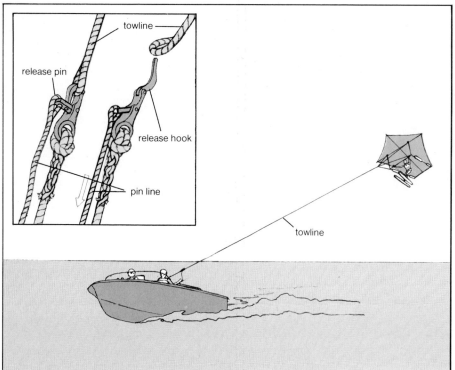

A properly rigged kite-skiing boat tows the airborne skier at the end
of a 100-foot-long, ⅜-inch towline attached to a quick-release device
(inset). One end of the release is secured to the boat's towing pylon,
and the line leading from the release pin is held by the observer, who
also controls the boat's speed. To begin the flight, the driver taxis
into the wind and the observer accelerates smoothly to a flying speed
of some 30 miles an hour. This provides the lift needed to get the
skier 10 to 30 feet into the air and keep him there. To end the flight,
the observer slows down until the skier alights on the water. He then
pulls the pin line, disengaging the skier from the boat.

Silhouetted against the sun, an airborne skier
firmly gripping his kite's trapeze bar hangs
from a safety harness above Biscayne Bay.
By shifting weight from one side of the bar
to the other he can control the kite's lateral
movement. His altitude is governed by the
speed of the boat, which he controls by
signals to the observer. For increased speed
—and altitude—he crosses his ski-tips; to
reduce altitude, he crosses the backs. At the
end of the flight, the skier is kept afloat by
his life vest, the kite by Styrofoam floats.

5 The ways of playing with the wind are as variable as the wind itself, and pushing a conventional displacement sailing hull through the water is only one of them. Sailors nowadays disport themselves in any number of wind-powered ways, such as skimming at three to five times the wind's speed across frozen lakes, soaring aloft on ballooning spinnakers and whizzing over desert sands on land-bound versions of the ubiquitous Sailfish. The acrobatic Californian at the left, for example, is demonstrating one of the most challenging and popular of the new crop of wind toys. Called a Windsurfer, it was created in 1967 by two southern Californians, one a computer expert and surf-

PLAYING WITH THE WIND

er, the other an aeronautical engineer and sailor. Looking for ways to extend the adventurous range of their sports, they designed the sailing rig shown here and overleaf, with a mast stepped on a universal joint and a wishbone boom. The device—and the sport—have caught on worldwide among enthusiasts, who find it the closest thing to becoming one with the wind.

Equally thrilling but somewhat more complex and expensive is spinnaker flying, which came into its own with the development of modern nylon spinnakers. Their combination of strength and lift allows a crew member swimming off the bow of a stern-anchored boat to grab a line slung along the foot of a partially hoisted spinnaker and then hang on—or pull himself up onto a trapeze-like seat—and ride with the rising sail as if he were a kite's tail.

Though wind surfing and spinnaker flying are very new, other ways that sportsmen by the tens of thousands are playing with wind date back to the earliest days of sail. Land sailing was first tried by the early Chinese, who rigged farm carts with sails. In 1600, a Dutch sail-wagon skipper took 26 breathless passengers 54 miles along a beach at an average of 27 miles per hour—a speed record for wheeled travel until after the invention of the steam locomotive. Throughout America's 19th Century westward expansion, various unembarrassable promoters tried to sell the concept of speeding across the Great Plains in elaborate land yachts. Today's land-sailing craft are of two major types. Most popular are the small, spindly vehicles, often home-built, that carry around 50 square feet of sail and have a top speed of close to 60 miles per hour. On a more professional level are the larger, custom-designed models carrying up to 150 square feet of sail and capable of approaching 80 miles per hour. And though the sport is not as popular in the U.S. as is wind surfing, it has adherents abroad. Not long ago, a French general led land yachtsmen from eight nations on a 1,500-mile race in the Sahara; the event reportedly ended with the cry of "Sea ho!" at the sight of the Atlantic after 32 days.

Even faster than land sailers are iceboats, which first gained popularity around 1860 on the frozen lakes and rivers of upstate New York. Though they sometimes carried commercial passengers and even livestock, their main appeal was as sport vehicles. At the turn of the century, iceboating had become a wintertime favorite of socially prominent families like the Roosevelts and Vanderbilts. Clubs in New York and New Jersey contended in regattas as elegant as Marblehead Race Week, and iceboaters on the frozen Hudson River used to outrun the New York Central's crack train, the Albany Flyer.

For all their speed, however, these early iceboats were ponderous affairs that weighed as much as 2,000 pounds, measured 30 to 50 feet in length and needed several hundred square feet of canvas to get them moving. Modern versions, like most of the other wind-driven devices that are shown on the subsequent pages, are light, simple, easily portable and—by conventional boating standards—inexpensive. But for pure adventure they can barely be matched by any earth-bound craft.

Leaning against the pull of his sail, an athletic Californian coaxes 12 knots out of his Windsurfer. A window in the sail lets him see to leeward, and the wet suit keeps him warm.

To raise the mast, the skipper stands on the board, which is positioned across the wind; her back is thus to the wind. With a firm grip on the uphaul line, she begins to lean back, keeping her back straight.

As the sail lifts from the water, she slowly but firmly pulls hand over hand on the uphaul. Note that the sail naturally turns head to wind, so that it comes up luffing.

When the sail is all the way up, the skipper lets go of the uphaul and takes a direct hold on the boom. Deciding to set off on port tack, she begins moving around the front of the mast to the port side, picking up what will be the windward side of the boom.

Using her forward hand as a windward shroud to hold the mast in an upright position, and her after hand as a sheet to trim the boom, the skipper begins sailing close-hauled.

Wind Surfing

The fastest-growing offshoot of conventional sailing is wind surfing. Requiring only inexpensive and portable equipment, the sport has quickly caught on with surfers and sailors—and people who had never tried either sport; there are thousands of wind surfers in the United States, Europe and Japan.

The Windsurfer is a 12-foot, 60-pound polyurethane board with a detachable, rotating mast (below); it also has a small centerboard and skeg, but no rudder. The skipper steers by changing the sail's position (right). The rig's simplicity and the skipper's nearness to the forces operating on him make learning to sail the craft fairly easy; veteran wind surfers claim they can teach a novice the basics in a day.

For many beginners, the hardest part of the learning process is raising the mast (left). Many would-be wind surfers clamber onto the board, lean back to raise the sail and fall backward into the water, bringing the sail over on top of them. But if the beginner keeps his back to the wind and concentrates on holding the mast perpendicular to the board's fore-and-aft axis as he raises it, he should be able to get safely underway on his second or third try.

Once the mast is up, the skipper trims the sail simply by adjusting his hold on the double boom. Tacking and jibing on a Windsurfer are easier than on a sailboat (overleaf), and capsizing is an event of no consequence to the novice—he merely finds himself in the water, the board and mast floating close beside him.

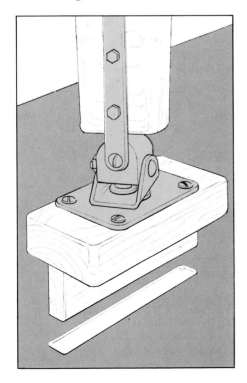

A Windsurfer's mast stands on a universal joint that allows it to swing in any direction. The joint, in turn, attaches to its own mounting, which fits into a slot on the board. Once in place, the mast can be raked forward or aft to steer, or can be pulled over to windward by a skipper hiking out—a tactic that stops the board from heeling. Without this latter capability, the light Windsurfer would capsize in the gentlest winds.

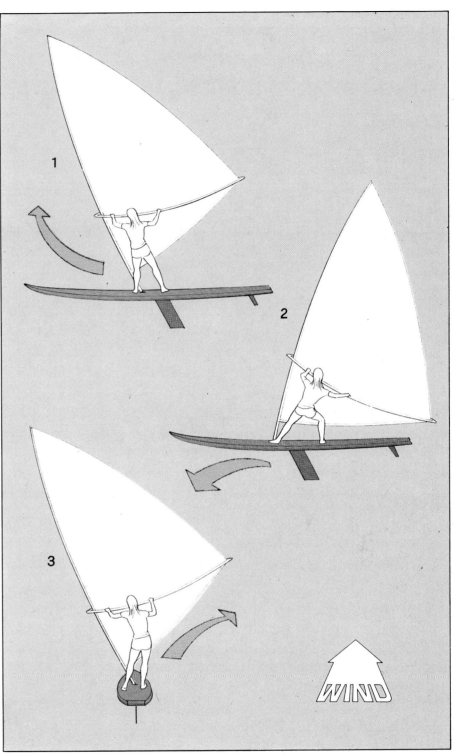

A Windsurfer is steered by changing the position of the sail's center of effort relative to the boat's center of lateral resistance—the centerboard. To head off the wind, the skipper rakes the mast forward (1): the wind pushes the bow to leeward. To head closer to the wind, the mast is raked aft (2), forcing the stern away from the wind and the bow toward it. To steer anywhere between a broad reach and a run, the mast is raked to windward or leeward. Raking to windward (3) turns the bow away from the wind; raking to leeward has the opposite effect.

THE TACK

To begin a tack, the skipper makes sure the Windsurfer is moving well, then rakes the mast aft to force the bow up into the wind.

She continues to keep raking pressure on the windward boom as the boat starts to come up into the wind and the sail begins to luff.

THE JIBE

To jibe a Windsurfer from a run, the skipper rakes the mast to windward so as to turn the bow away from the wind. (A jibe from a reach would be initiated by raking the mast forward.)

As the stern of the craft passes through the wind, the skipper releases the outside hand on the boom and allows the sail to swing forward.

When the boat is head to wind, sail luffing, the skipper moves quickly around the front of the mast and picks up the new windward boom.

She then rakes the mast forward in order to force the bow of the Windsurfer to bear off on the new tack. When the bow is at least 45° off the wind, she will bring the mast back to center.

When the sail, blown by the wind, crosses the centerline of the Windsurfer, the skipper picks up the new windward boom.

She then trims the sail to pick up speed, raking the rig slightly aft, if necessary, to put the Windsurfer on course on the new tack.

Racing Windsurfers approach a mark in the national championships
regatta in San Diego, California. Although wind surfing is essentially
recreational, competitive wind surfing has rapidly taken hold, with
fleets of as many as 200 competing for national and world titles.
At these and other major regattas, skippers are divided into classes by
their weight, since in extreme weather conditions weight can be a
critical factor in performance. In light air, a 100-pound sailor will slip
ahead of his 170-pound rival; in stronger winds, heavier sailors have
an advantage in being able to keep their craft properly balanced.

A wave-riding wind surfer off Hawaii hangs far out for balance as his
board skims across the crest of a small roller. Surfers like this one first
sail their boards out to where the waves begin to curl, then turn and,
getting a combined boost from wind and sea, ride the surf back in.
For better control in strong winds, this acrobatic sailor has traded his
standard sail for a storm sail that is 16 square feet smaller.

Spinnaker Flying

Cruising sailors who have anchored in a breezy cove may want to try spinnaker flying, a spectacular new sport that is easier and safer than it looks. The only requirements are a mast that is 35 feet or more high, a 10- to 20-knot breeze, and a little bit of nerve.

To set up for spinnaker flying, the crew first anchors the boat by the stern so that the bow faces downwind. A heavy anchor should be used and plenty of line let out to prevent the boat from dragging against the pull of the sail. The spinnaker should be checked for any weaknesses at the clews or along seams; as long as the sail is in good shape, spinnaker flying will not hurt it—the strains will be less severe than on an afternoon's sail.

After the spinnaker passes inspection it can quickly be rigged for flight. First the halyard is attached to the head. Then a second line, about as long as the foot of the sail, is made fast to each clew; the rider uses this line to hang on to, and to trim the sail. Some riders hang directly on the line. Others rig a wood or canvas bosun's chair to the line, using a small block or ring so that they can slide along the line once they are in the air. Finally, a long retriever, or trip line, is run from one clew of the sail to a cleat on the foredeck, so that a crewman can spill wind from the sail and haul the rig back to the boat if the breeze suddenly gets too gusty.

When these lines have been rigged, one crew member hoists the spinnaker *(far right)*, the rider swims out to the sail and the ride begins.

Confidently upright on a bosun's chair, a woman goes spinnaker flying off Miami, Florida. Daring riders, like the one above, can swoop from side to side by pulling on the line between the clews. In a strong and gusty wind, the spinnaker may rise up until it flies almost horizontal—whereupon it spills air and drops as much as 20 feet, before rising again in a breathtaking roller-coaster action.

A flight like the one in the photograph at left begins when a crew member raises the halyard partway up, until the head of the spinnaker floats just forward of the tip of the bow. Then the rider swims out to the bosun's chair, climbs in, and trims the line to the clews until the sail fills and lifts him into the air. When the rider is ready to come down, he can either pull on the line to one of the clews, thus slowly collapsing the sail, or call to a crew member on deck to pull on the retriever line. At no time should the crew haul the spinnaker to the masthead; the rider might swing in and hit the boat.

Land Sailing

Land Sailing

A fleet of land sailers—some commercially built, others designed and constructed by their owners—wheels across a dry lake bed near Las Vegas. Land-sailing clubs were established in Florida and the West, where beaches, deserts and lake beds offer sufficient open level ground. Equipped with a single sail and foot-pedal steering, these small land sailers travel up to three times the speed of the wind.

THE INTOXICATING SPEED OF ICEBOATING

During the months when most boating enthusiasts are beached and waiting for warmer temperatures, some 4,000 iceboaters are chafing in readiness for the biting cold, clear days that will produce the perfect conditions for their sport. In the course of an entire season, iceboaters may get only a few weekends of good sailing, but with four inches of hard, smooth ice and a 10-knot breeze, the exhilaration of high speed makes all of the waiting worthwhile.

In good conditions, an iceboat can rocket across a frozen lake at 50 to 100 miles per hour. With the wind roaring by, iceboating becomes much like flying in a small, open aircraft. In fact, iceboaters have adopted certain aviation terminology: they call an iceboat's long, narrow hull a fuselage. And the sail, moving sometimes five times faster than the natural breeze on the lake, pulls the boat powerfully forward in a precise, landbound analogy of the function of an airplane wing.

Fast-paced as it is, iceboating does not rank among the most dangerous sports, and participants receive far fewer injuries than do skiers. A major reason is that iceboaters approach their sport with caution: they are careful to check the thickness of the ice before going out, and only rarely does an improvident soul need to be fished from a patch of open water. Aware of the risks of collision, iceboaters adhere strictly to right-of-way rules.

Iceboaters also take great care to avoid frostbite. Most wear thermal underwear, several layers of clothing, a quilted warm-up suit, gloves, hat, helmet, and boots with cleats called creepers to give them traction on the ice.

Despite the hazards and the long waits for the right weather, iceboaters are a loyal lot and would not trade their sport for any other—including the summer counterpart, which they call with friendly condescension "soft-water sailing."

A crash-helmeted iceboat sailor shoots across a frozen lake at
40 miles per hour as his runners kick up powder from a thin layer of
snow. Iceboats can slice through snow one or two inches deep;
a thicker covering will bury the blades and slow the boat to a stop.

A Spectrum of Iceboats

Sunfish on the Rocks

Anyone with a Sailfish or Sunfish rig in his garage is halfway to owning an iceboat. A number of marine dealers produce inexpensive hulls made of galvanized tubular steel and designed to accommodate the sail of either of these two popular board boats. And a handy boatman may even build his own, using wood for the hull and angle iron for runners. Though the resulting boat may reach speeds of no more than about 40 mph, its large, full sail makes it quick to accelerate in breezes too light for other iceboats.

The Arrow, one of several production-built, one-design iceboats, is 16 feet long and carries 80 square feet of sail. Its cockpit is designed to seat two people side by side, making it an excellent family boat.

The largest iceboats are the Class A's; many are gaff-rigged stern-steerers built in the late 1800s and still raced in regattas like this one at Red Bank, New Jersey. Weighing almost 2,000 pounds, they can carry 750 square feet of sail and reach speeds of 70 mph or better.

The fastest iceboat—capable of about 120 mph—is the Class E, or Skeeter. Since the only class rule is an upper limit on sail area (75 square feet), skippers may experiment with everything else—the height and rake of the mast, the length of the plank between runners or the streamlining of the hull. Most Skeeters are about 25 feet long and have a 24-foot mast and an 18-foot runner plank.

The 12-foot DN, which can travel up to 60 mph under 60 square feet of sail, is the most popular of all iceboats—despite an open cockpit so slender that the skipper just fits in it, leaning back against a stubby rest. More than 3,000 of these lightweight, easily transportable boats have been built, and national regattas draw as many as 100 boats.

Designed to a T

The development of iceboat design has led to a single basic shape, exemplified by the one-design Yankee-class Skeeter at right. Like others among the modern crop of fast, maneuverable craft, the Yankee is T-shaped: the long, narrow hull and front steering-runner assembly form the base of the T, and the crosspiece connecting the two side runners forms the top. The craft is driven by a single small, flat sail hoisted on a streamlined, rotating mast.

This shape was arrived at after decades of thundering along in old-style iceboats, which were inverted Ts with the steering runner at the stern—an arrangement that created serious problems. Since the center of effort of the sail was far forward over the side runners, wind pressure often lifted the steering runner off the ice, causing the boat to spin out of control.

The solution, moving the steering runner from stern to bow, was arrived at by Wisconsin sailors in the 1930s. Control improved so dramatically that soon new bow steerers were beating older boats carrying more than four times the sail area.

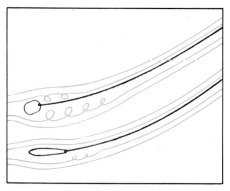

The advantages of a rotating, streamlined mast are shown in these drawings. At top, a stream of air hitting an ordinary fixed mast —such as is found on most sailboats— separates into eddies of disturbed air. But the tear-shaped mast, which rotates so that its long axis coincides with the sail's leading edge, allows a smooth flow of air that may add as much as one third to the sail's power.

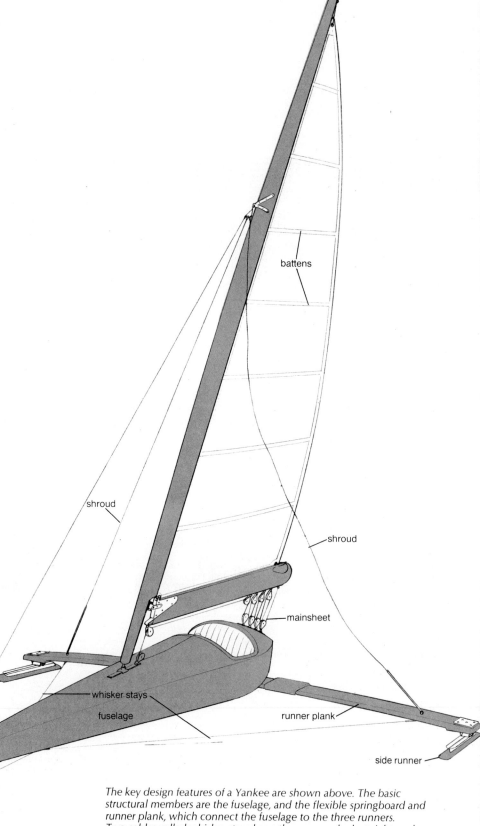

The key design features of a Yankee are shown above. The basic structural members are the fuselage, and the flexible springboard and runner plank, which connect the fuselage to the three runners. Two cables called whisker stays keep the runner plank at right angles to the hull. The driving force is a small mainsail fitted with full-length battens to give the sail its airfoil shape. The shrouds carry considerable play so that the rig can tip to leeward, exerting a downward pressure on the leeward runner to help keep the boat from sliding sideways. And since iceboats are sensitive to any random breeze, the front runner carries a flip-down parking brake.

The base assembly of the mast is the key to efficient sail trim. A ball joint allows the mast to rotate to line up with the airfoil shape of the sail, and also to move from side to side to take up slack in the windward shroud when the boat tacks. The ball joint can be moved to keep the center of effort of the sail in the optimum spot. Just behind the ball joint is the ratchet block used to trim the mainsheet.

A multiple-block system (here eight blocks) on the mainsheet gives the skipper the mechanical advantage he needs to trim the sail—both in and down (the boom has no downhaul). The mainsheet leads from this web of blocks forward to a block at the gooseneck and then down to the ratchet block before running back to the skipper. Thus, after the skipper has hauled the boom close amidships, he can take unwanted draft out of the sail with another tug on the sheet.

The steering runner is rigged to wire cables that lead back to the cockpit. This runner, like the side runners, is made of case-hardened steel and mounted on a bolt that allows it to pivot to ride over any rough spots on the ice. The runners are kept sharpened to an angle of between 80° and 100°, depending on the condition of the ice.

A Yankee is steered basically by a wheel connected to the front runner by cables. Under the deck are auxiliary foot pedals that the skipper uses to steer at times when he needs his hands free to trim the mainsheet. Smaller boats like the DN and Arrow have a front-pivoting tiller instead of a wheel—and no foot pedals. Skippers can control the tiller with their knees when they are working sheets.

Subtle Art of Sail Trim

Despite their narrow cockpits and astonishing speeds, iceboats are really not harder to handle than most sailboats. An iceboat sails upwind in much the same way a sailboat does, but in light air or on rough or snowy ice a skipper can increase his speed by heading down about 10° —and more than make up for the extra distance sailed. If he hits a puff and the boat hikes more than a foot off the ice —an action that spills wind and slows the boat—the skipper does just what he would do in a sailboat: he eases the sheet or heads closer to the wind.

On a reach, a skipper adjusts the sheet or heads down to correct hiking, but because of his speed, his greatest concern is with safety. To avoid an obstruction, or another boat, he needs plenty of clear ice ahead to make a turn or to luff to a stop.

Going off the wind, iceboaters avoid making a dead run, which greatly slows the craft. Instead, they sail in a series of broad reaches. Jibing through these reaches is easier than on a sailboat; since an iceboat travels faster than the wind, a jibe is similar to a tack.

The biggest handling difference between an iceboat and a sailboat relates to sail trim. The drawings at right take an iceboat through a full circle, showing the boat's preferred course, the direction of the apparent wind, and the position of the mainsail for each point of sailing.

This special telltale mounted on the front of an iceboat's rotating mast is used by some skippers to help judge how well they are managing their boats relative to the wind. If a skipper can keep the telltale's fin pointing to the middle of the mast, he is sure that the wind is flowing properly on both sides of the sail. If the telltale points to windward, he knows that air is reaching only the windward side of the sail, and that the sail is stalled. To correct this condition, he heads up slightly. If the telltale points to leeward of the mast, he is heading too high, and should bear off.

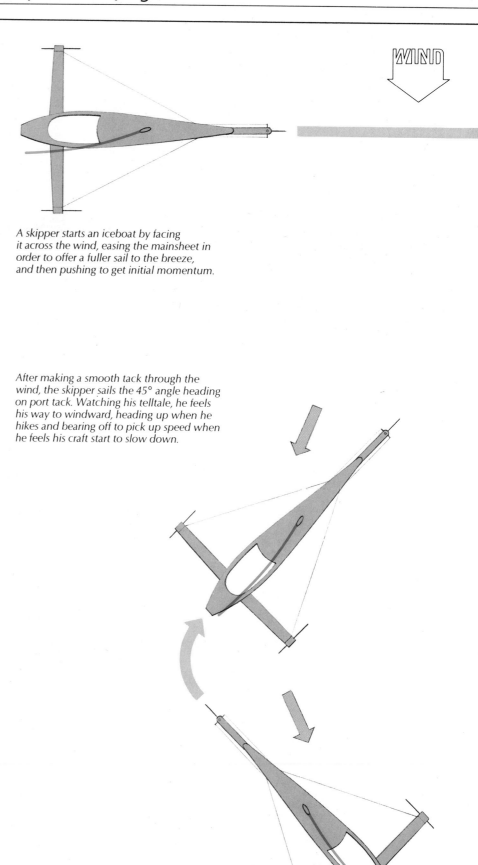

A skipper starts an iceboat by facing it across the wind, easing the mainsheet in order to offer a fuller sail to the breeze, and then pushing to get initial momentum.

After making a smooth tack through the wind, the skipper sails the 45° angle heading on port tack. Watching his telltale, he feels his way to windward, heading up when he hikes and bearing off to pick up speed when he feels his craft start to slow down.

As he heads up to a close-hauled course, the skipper sails at about 45° to the true wind and at about 18° to the apparent wind— approximately 10° closer to the apparent wind than a sailboat can point.

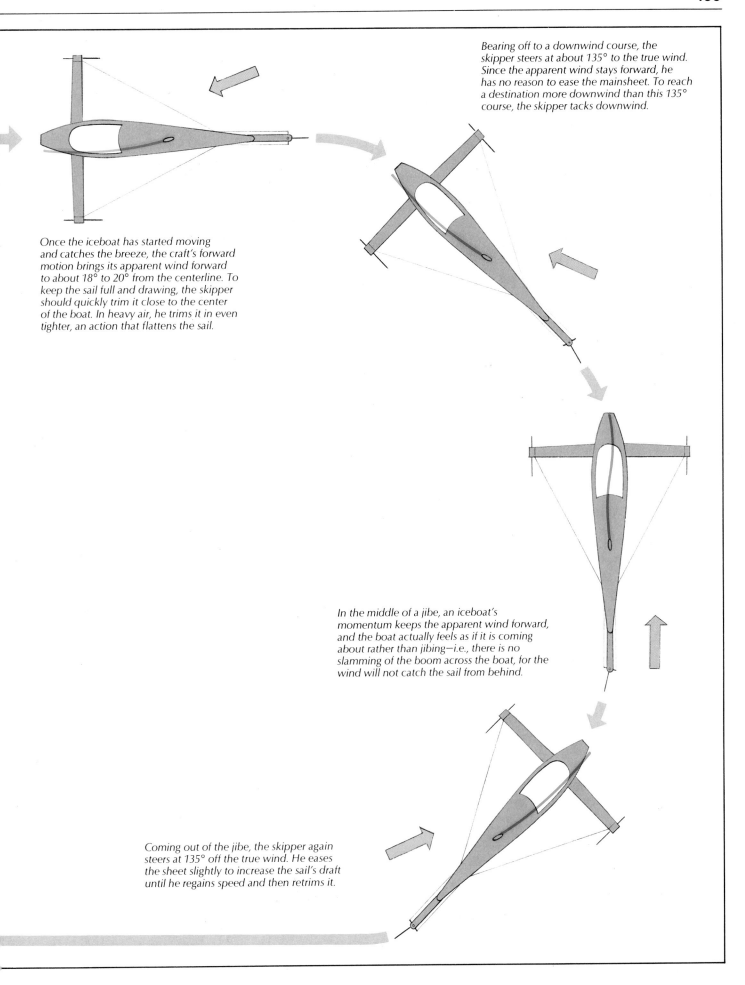

Bearing off to a downwind course, the skipper steers at about 135° to the true wind. Since the apparent wind stays forward, he has no reason to ease the mainsheet. To reach a destination more downwind than this 135° course, the skipper tacks downwind.

Once the iceboat has started moving and catches the breeze, the craft's forward motion brings its apparent wind forward to about 18° to 20° from the centerline. To keep the sail full and drawing, the skipper should quickly trim it close to the center of the boat. In heavy air, he trims it in even tighter, an action that flattens the sail.

In the middle of a jibe, an iceboat's momentum keeps the apparent wind forward, and the boat actually feels as if it is coming about rather than jibing—i.e., there is no slamming of the boom across the boat, for the wind will not catch the sail from behind.

Coming out of the jibe, the skipper again steers at 135° off the true wind. He eases the sheet slightly to increase the sail's draft until he regains speed and then retrims it.

The Ultimate Test

Some iceboat sailors find a satisfaction in making timed runs over a measured course in an attempt to break speed records, but most prefer to match their skill against other skippers in regattas or single races. On weekends when there is ice at a place like Connecticut's Bantam Lake, for example, DN and Skeeter sailors squeeze in four or five races in an afternoon. For these informal club races, they set out marks and call their own starts, with the faster Skeeters sailing more times around the course as a handicap.

Iceboaters everywhere sail a windward-leeward course, since on the reaches of a triangular course boats might hike dangerously. All races begin with the skippers shoving their boats in a running start. The severest test of skill is on the leeward leg. While heading as close as possible to the mark, skippers try to hold to the optimum angle of 135° to the true wind. When the wind dies, they head up 10° or 20° to maintain speed, then head down through gusts. They jibe at least once on every leeward leg, and a key decision is when to jibe for the mark. A skipper who jibes too early either will have to jibe again, or will head so far downwind that his sail will lose its efficiency; he may even stop.

But iceboating's rules allow a stalled skipper to get out and push his boat to get started again. The rules offer another departure from those used in soft-water racing: on a downwind leg, a windward iceboat has right of way over a leeward one on the same tack, since if the windward boat hikes, it will need room to bear off to come down again.

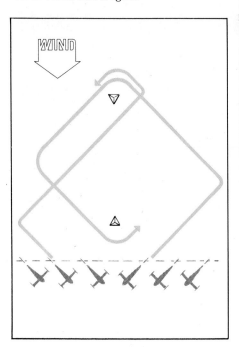

A typical iceboat race follows the windward-leeward pattern shown at left. In large fleets, half of the boats line up for the start on port tack at 45° from the wind; the other half line up on starboard. (In smaller fleets, all boats may line up on the same tack.) They then beat upwind, making only a single tack if there is enough clear ice to do so; a series of tacks would keep them closer to the mark but would cost too much in speed. Finally, they tack downwind, jibing one or more times to reach the leeward mark. The course is sailed two or three times around, and finished at the leeward mark.

DN skippers push their boats to start a race beneath squall clouds threatening to drop more snow on the heavily dusted ice of Bantam Lake. Although a running start requires less tactical maneuvering than does a sailboat start, the scurrying skipper must know precisely the right time to jump aboard and trim sail. If he jumps too soon, he may find himself sailing slower than he could run. If he jumps too late, a competitor will have accelerated ahead, then found clear air —an advantage likely to be held for the remainder of the leg.

An iceboat skipper sailing upwind watches the boat ahead of him hike —a sign that a gust is on the way. Since iceboaters have no water to windward to provide clues of wind to come, they watch other boats. Forewarned, this Skeeter sailor can head up to avoid hiking, and thus get a lift in speed by making more efficient use of the wind.

A DN with a Skeeter hard on its heels rounds the leeward mark, hiking slightly as the true wind comes abeam. To prevent the speed loss that results from excessive hiking, iceboaters often ease the mainsheet as they turn a mark, and then retrim for the windward leg.

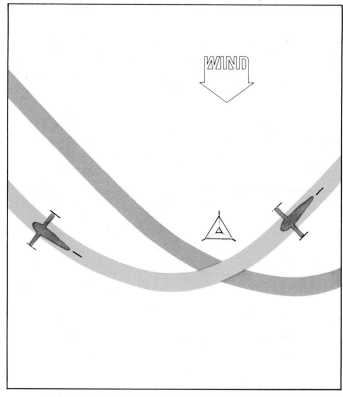

When an iceboat skipper swoops down on a leeward mark, as those right are doing, he tries to begin his turn wide of the mark (blue line) and then swing in close to it. Thus, even if his boat hikes and skids to leeward, he can still shave the mark close on the far side, putting himself as far to windward as possible for the next leg. If he cuts the mark too close on the approach (gray line), he comes out of the turn in a less favorable position—to leeward and behind.

A DN sailor heading for home after a race kicks up an explosion of snow with his craft's leeward runner.

Glossary

Abeam A direction at right angles to the centerline of the boat.

Apparent wind The wind that blows across a boat, composed of a combination of true wind and wind created by the boat's forward motion.

Backwater To move a rowboat or canoe backward by pushing the oars or paddles so that the blades move through the water from aft forward.

Bait well A well or tank aboard ship, in which sea water or fresh water circulates —or through which air bubbles are passed —to keep bait alive when fishing; also called a live-bait well.

Battens Flexible strips of wood or fiberglass placed in a sail's leech to help the sail's trailing edge retain its proper shape.

Bear off To turn a boat away from the direction of the wind.

Bimini top An overhead sunshade used to shelter an open bridge, most typically on a sport-fishing boat. It was originally used on the waters off the big-game-fishing center of Bimini, the Bahamas.

Block A wood or metal shell enclosing one or more sheaves, through which lines are led.

Bridle Portion of a water-ski towline—including the handle—held by the skier and leading to the after end of the main towline; also, a short length of extra-strong rope made fast at either end to the towing eyes on a boat's transom, and used to hold the forward end of a ski towline clear of the towboat's engine.

Broach A boat is said to broach when it swerves and heels dangerously, so that the hull turns broadside to the waves and is in danger of capsizing or foundering.

Cannonball The weight on a downrigger that holds a trolled lure at a chosen depth.

Cathedral A hull configuration with sponsons on either side of a narrow center hull.

Cartopping The act of transporting a boat on the top of a car, usually by attaching it to a roof rack.

Center of effort (CE) A theoretical point on a boat's sail plan that represents the focus or center of the total forces of wind on the sails.

Center of lateral resistance (CLR) A point below a boat's waterline representing the focus or pivot point of the total hydrodynamic forces on the hull.

Chute A short section of a river consisting of a relatively steep drop down a narrow channel; also, colloquial for spinnaker —a lightweight headsail set from a boat that is reaching or running before the wind.

Clew The lower after corner of a sail, where the foot meets the leech.

Climbing the pole A hand-over-hand technique used in poling a craft over flats or upstream.

Close-hauled A boat is close-hauled when its sails are trimmed in tight and it is heading as close to the wind as it can while still keeping its speed.

Console A compact mechanical unit, typically housed in a cabinet, in which are mounted an engine's throttle, starter button, steering wheel and other equipment related to the control of a boat.

Counter The after portion of a hull from the waterline to the extreme end of the overhang.

Cuddy cabin A small cabin, usually placed well forward and containing spartan living and stowage facilities.

Deadrise The angle at which the bottom rises, from where it joins the keel to the turn of the bilge, or chine.

Depth finder An instrument for measuring the depth of the water by means of a timed sonic pulse; also known as depth sounder or echo sounder.

Displacement The weight of the water displaced by a floating boat. It is equal to the weight of the boat.

Double boom The paired, curved booms that run along the leeward and windward sides of a Windsurfer's sail; sometimes called a twin control boom or a wishbone boom.

Double wake cut An S-curve maneuver by which a water-ski jumper builds up centrifugal force to acquire speed significantly greater than that of the towboat.

Downrigger A device mounted on the gunwale of a boat designed to hold a trolled lure at a precise depth and to release it when a fish strikes.

Draft The depth a vessel extends below the waterline; the position and amount of maximum camber in a sail.

Eddy A backwater in a river, occurring directly downstream from an obstruction to the current.

Entrance The immersed forebody of a hull from the extreme forward waterline to the point where the hull reaches its widest or deepest section; also called the entry.

Eskimo roll A technique used by kayak paddlers to right an overturned craft through a combination of paddle stroke and body movement.

Eye splice A permanent loop made at a rope's end by weaving unlaid strands into the standing part of the line.

Fairlead An eye or block—usually attached to a deck—that guides a line in a desired direction.

Feather To turn an oar blade after the pulling stroke so that it rests or moves nearly parallel to the water, and offers the least possible resistance to wind and waves.

Fighting chair A sturdy swiveling chair with a foot brace, bolted solidly to the cockpit sole and used by an angler when playing big game fish.

Fish door A sturdy door set into the transom of a sport fisherman and opened briefly as a convenience when boating a large fish.

Fish finder A fisherman's term for a depth finder, deriving from the fact that the instrument's sonic pulses can pinpoint the location of schools of fish—and sometimes of individual fish.

Fishing chair A sturdy chair, either fixed or portable, with no foot brace, used for trolling or fighting small fish.

Flying bridge A raised platform, usually located on a powerboat's cabin top and equipped with a control console.

Forefoot The forward portion of a boat where the stem meets the keel.

Freeboard The vertical distance measured on the boat's side from the waterline to the deck.

Fuselage The hull of an iceboat.

Gaff A spar to support and spread the head of a sail of four generally unequal sides; also, a sturdy pole with a hook on one end, used for pulling hooked fish aboard. A flying gaff has a hook that detaches from the pole but remains fixed to a line whose other end is hand-held or made fast to a cleat.

Galley A seagoing kitchen.

Gin pole A fixed pole equipped with a block and tackle, and mounted vertically on a fishing boat to hoist heavy fish aboard.

Grab rail A securely mounted handhold on or below deck.

Grapnel A small anchor with four or five hooklike tines, used for anchoring or in dragging or grappling operations.

Guide buoys Pairs of marker buoys set down to indicate the path a skier's towboat must take in competition runs.

Gunwale The rail around the outer rim of a boat's deck or cockpit.

Guy The windward spinnaker sheet, used to control the spinnaker pole.

Hatch An opening in the deck giving access below; also, its cover.

Hawsepipe A metal fitting that acts as a deck fairlead for docking lines. Some are convertible into fishing-rod holders.

Haystacks See Standing wave.

Head down To steer a boat away from the direction of the wind.

Head up To steer a boat in the direction of the wind.

Heel A sideways leaning of a boat caused by the wind's force on the sails.

Helm The device—usually a tiller or wheel, attached or connected to the rudder—by which a boat is steered.

Hike A sideways leaning of an iceboat.

Hike out To extend one's body outboard of a sailing boat's gunwales in an effort to keep the craft on a more even keel.

Honey hole An underwater spot where an unusual number of hungry game fish are said to be.

Inboard Toward a boat's centerline; also, a common contraction for a boat with an inboard engine.

Inboard engine An engine permanently mounted inside a boat's hull.

Inflatable Any of a variety of air-filled collapsible craft used for sport fishing and river touring, and as life rafts and tenders for larger craft.

Jibe To turn a sailboat's stern through the wind so that the sails swing from one side of the boat to the other, thus putting the boat on another tack.

Johnboat A small, flat-bottomed shallow-draft boat, square at bow and stern, commonly used for fishing.

Leeboard A wood or metal board, usually one of a pair, attached to the sides or, like a centerboard, through the hull outboard of the cockpit to prevent leeway.

Leeward In the direction away from the wind (pronounced LOO-ard).

Luff The leading edge of the sail; also, the fluttering of a sail when the boat is pointed too close to the wind or when the sail is let out too far; also, to head up.

Lure Artificial bait used for catching fish.

Outboard Out from the hull, or toward the outside away from the centerline; also, a contraction for outboard motor or for a boat with an outboard motor.

Outboard motor An engine mounted with clamps outside a boat's hull.

Outrigger A pole—usually one of a pair—mounted on a fishing boat, used to raise a fishing line high above the water and extend it outboard of the boat's wake.

Painter A bow line for a small boat.

Parking brake On an iceboat, a flip-down device used to hold the boat in place, preventing it from drifting off downwind when the skipper is not aboard.

Pay out To slack a line so that it runs out.

Pin line A lanyard used to trip the hook of a quick release for kite skiers.

Portage The act of carrying a boat or goods overland around stream obstructions or between two waterways.

Pulpit A strong railing at the bow or stern of boats to prevent crew members from going overboard; also, a railed platform extending forward from the bow of a sport fisherman, used as a vantage point for sighting, spearing or gaffing fish.

Pylon A sturdy pole or tripod mounted on a water-ski boat as the on-board terminal for a towline.

Quick-release clip A device that holds a fishing line to the tip of an outrigger or downrigger when trolling and releases it the moment a fish strikes so that the fish can be played by the angler.

Rake As a noun, the inclination from the perpendicular (usually aft) of the mast of a sailboat; as a verb, to increase that inclination.

Ramp An inclined plane on the shore used for hauling and launching boats; an inclined plane in the water used by water-ski jumpers as a take-off point.

Riffles A succession of small waves extending across the surface of shallow water in a stream bed.

Rip Turbulence created by a swift current, usually in tidal water, flowing over an irregular bottom.

Rock garden A scattering of rocks and boulders that creates rapids in a river's channel.

Rode An anchor line.

Run The afterbody of a hull, from the point at which the hull's bulk begins to diminish.

Runabout A small, lightweight motorboat

with an open cockpit.

Scupper A hole or opening in a rail, hatch or ventilator to allow water to drain off.

Semi-V A hull shape, part of which (typically the entrance) is V-shaped and part (typically the run) flat; also called the modified V.

Sheer The curve of a boat's rail from stem to stern.

Shrouds Ropes or wires led from the mast to chain plates at deck level on either side of the mast. They hold the mast from falling or bending sideways.

Slalom A type of water-skiing or kayaking in which the water sportsman weaves back and forth over a prescribed course.

Snubbing Stopping or slowing a canoe's momentum with a pole while traveling downstream; stopping a line from running out by taking turnings around a cleat, bitt, piling or similar stationary object.

Sounding The water depth at a given spot, measured in feet or fathoms; a chart notation of water depth at mean low water; the act of measuring water depth with a lead line or a depth finder.

Souse hole A depression in the surface of a river formed where water pours over the downstream side of a barely submerged rock, creating an eddy.

Spinnaker A full-bellied, lightweight sail set forward of the mast on a spinnaker pole and normally carried when a sailboat is reaching or running.

Spinnaker pole A long, light, portable spar used to extend the foot of a spinnaker.

Sponson A pontoon-like structure protruding from the side of a hull, usually to increase buoyancy and stability.

Spray skirt A nylon covering attached snugly to a kayak's cockpit to form a watertight seal around the paddler.

Standing wave A wave formed by water piling at the end of a fast-flowing chute, causing a succession of three or four stationary crests; also known as haystacks.

Stern drive A system of power propulsion in which an inboard engine drives a propeller unit that resembles the lower unit of an outboard in appearance and function; sometimes called inboard-outboard, or I-O.

Surfing Traveling down the forward face of a wave so as to increase a boat's speed.

Tachometer An instrument indicating the number of revolutions per minute (rpm's) at which an engine is turning.

Tack To alter a boat's course through the eye of the wind; also, the lower forward corner of a sail.

Tackle In fishing, the hand-held equipment that is used by an angler, e.g., rod, line, hook, sinker; also, a line run through a set of blocks so as to gain a mechanical advantage in raising or lowering a heavy object.

Teaser A large, hookless, metal trolling lure trailed behind a fishing boat to help attract game fish.

Telltale A piece of yarn tied to shrouds or sails to indicate the direction of the apparent wind.

Thermocline The region of abrupt temperature transition between the warm upper layers and the cold lower layers in a body of water.

Thermometer/depth gauge An instrument lowered overboard to record the temperature of the water and its depth at the spot to which it has been lowered.

Thwart A crosswise bar for structural support in an open boat.

Tow hitch A mechanical device such as a bridle or pylon for attaching a water-ski towline to a towboat.

Towing eye A heavy-duty U bolt on the transom of a boat for attaching a ski-tow bridle.

Towline The line that a water-skier holds when being pulled behind a boat.

Transducer The sending-receiving device of a depth finder that transmits sonic pulses to the bottom and then picks up the echoes.

Transom The flat aftermost part of a boat's stern.

Trawler A boat used in trawling, or commercial fishing with a net; a pleasure boat designed along the same lines.

Tricking The act of performing acrobatics on water skis.

Trolling To fish by pulling a baited hook and line through the water behind the boat.

Trolling motor A small, lightweight outboard motor, usually electrically powered, used for propelling a small craft slowly through a fishing area.

Tuna tower A tall structure topped by a platform, installed above the midship section of an offshore sport fisherman and used for spotting fish—particularly, large species such as tuna.

Turn of the bilge The curve where the bottom of a boat meets the topsides.

Uphaul The line that raises the mast on a Windsurfer.

Wake Disturbance of the surface of the water caused by a boat's passage.

Wet suit A close-fitting garment, usually made of neoprene, that serves to insulate the body from cold water.

Whip off On water skis, to cut across the towboat's wake in such a manner as to gain speed, and then to drop the towline and coast to a landing place.

Whisker stays Two cables that keep the runner plank on an iceboat at right angles to the hull.

White water Rapids.

Windsurfer A polyurethane surfboard with a detachable mast that rotates on a universal joint.

Windward The direction toward the wind source.

Wishbone boom See Double boom.

Bibliography

Fishing

Adams, Leon D., *Striped Bass Fishing*. Pacific Books, 1961.

Gennaro, Andy, *Trout Fishing*. The Fisherman Publishing Company, 1975.

Harbour, Dave, *Super Freshwater Fishing Systems*. The Stackpole Company, 1971.

Livingston, A. D., *Fishing for Bass: Modern Tactics and Tackle*. J. B. Lippincott Company, 1974.

McClane, A. J., editor, *McClane's Standard Fishing Encyclopedia and International Angling Guide*. Holt, Rinehart and Winston, 1965.

Mann, Tom, *Tom Mann's Secrets of the Bass Pros*. Bass Anglers Sportsman Society of America, Inc., 1976.

Moss, Frank T.:
Successful Ocean Game Fishing. International Marine Publishing Company, 1971.
Successful Striped Bass Fishing. International Marine Publishing Company, 1974.

1975 World Record Marine Fishes. International Game Fish Association, 1975.

Reiger, Z., *Zane Grey: Outdoorsman*. Prentice-Hall, 1972.

Rosko, Milt, *Fishing from Boats*. The Macmillan Company, 1968.

Woolner, Frank, *Modern Saltwater Sport Fishing*. Crown Publishers, Inc., 1972.

Canoeing

Adney, Edwin Tappan, and Howard I. Chapelle, *The Bark Canoes and Skin Boats of North America*. Smithsonian Institution, 1964.

Basic Canoeing. The American National Red Cross, 1965.

Bearse, Ray, *The Canoe Camper's Handbook*. Winchester Press, 1974.

Cheney, Theodore A., *Camping by Backpack and Canoe*. Funk & Wagnalls, 1970.

Durant, Kenneth, editor, *Guide-Boat Days and Ways*. Adirondack Museum, 1963.

Evans, Jay, and Robert R. Anderson, *Kayaking*. The Stephen Greene Press, 1975.

McNair, Robert E., *Basic River Canoeing*. American Camping Association Inc., 1968.

Malo, John, *Malo's Complete Guide to Canoeing and Canoe-Camping*. Quadrangle/The New York Times Book Co., 1974.

Michaelson, Mike, and Keith Ray, *Canoeing*. Henry Regnery Company, 1975.

Powell, J. W., *The Exploration of the Colorado River and Its Canyons*. Dover Publications, Inc., 1961.

Pulling, Pierre, *Principles of Canoeing*. The Macmillan Company, 1954.

Riviere, Bill, *Pole, Paddle & Portage*. Van Nostrand Reinhold Company, 1969.

Urban, John T., *A White Water Handbook for Canoe and Kayak*. Appalachian Mountain Club, 1974.

Wessels, William L., *Adirondack Profiles*. Adirondack Resorts Press, Inc., 1961.

Water-Skiing

Andresen, Jack, *Skiing on Water*. The Ronald Press Company, 1960.

Athans, George, Jr., and Clint Ward, *Water Skiing*. St. Martin's Press, 1975.

Bartlett, Tommy, *Tommy Bartlett's Guide to Water Skiing*. Chilton Company (Book Division, 1959.

Hardman, Thomas C., and William D. Clifford, *Let's Go Water Skiing*. Hawthorn Books, Inc., 1976.

Prince, Walter N., *Water Skiing for All*. Chilton Company (Book Division, 1959.

Scharff, Robert, *The Complete Book of Water Skiing*. G. P. Putnam's Sons, 1959.

Stephens, Kenneth, *Waterskiing*. McGraw-Hill Ryerson Limited, 1974.

Tyll, Al, *Water Skiing*. Arco Publishing Company, 1966.

Iceboating

Andresen, Jack, *Sailing on Ice*. A. S. Barnes and Company, 1974.

Gougeon, Meade, and Ty Knoy, *The Evolution of Modern Sailboat Design*. Winchester Press, 1973.

Levy, Natalie, "Offbeat Sailing." *Sail*, May 1974.

Yeager, John, "Spinnaker Flying." *Motorboating & Sailing*, July 1974.

Special Periodicals

BASSMASTER Magazine, Bass Anglers Sportsman Society of America, Inc., Montgomery, Alabama.

Canoe, American Canoe Association, Denver, Colorado.

Field & Stream, CBS Publications, New York City.

International Gamefisherman, International Gamefisherman, Inc., Miami, Florida.

Outdoor Life, Times Mirror Magazines, New York City.

Sportfishing, Yachting Publishing Corporation, New York City.

The Water Skier, American Water Ski Association, Winter Haven, Florida.

Wilderness Camping, United States Canoe Association, Schenectady, New York.

Acknowledgments

Portions of this book were written by Peter Wood. The index was prepared by Anita R. Beckerman. The editors also wish to thank the following: Tony Aeschliman, vice president, Horton, Church & Goff Inc.-Advertising, Providence, Rhode Island; Calvin Albury, Ocean Reef Club, Upper Key Largo, Florida; William Aucoin, Public Relations Representative, Johnson Motors, Waukegan, Illinois; William Beynon, Ocean Reef Club, Upper Key Largo, Florida; George and Robin Blair, Red Bank, New Jersey; Joan Borden, Public Relations Representative, Horton, Church & Goff Inc.-Advertising, Providence, Rhode Island; Winton Boyd, West Palm Beach, Florida; Davis Bragg, Killeen, Texas; Bob Cobb, editor, *BASSMASTER Magazine,* Montgomery, Alabama; Gail Cowart, Chicago, Illinois; Warren Darress, Port Washington, New York; Maitland DeSormo, Saranac Lake, New York; Bud Duncan, Killeen, Texas; George and Cookie Dyer, Lufkin, Texas; Deane Gray, Old Town Canoe Co., Old Town, Maine; Jeff Guertler, West Palm Beach, Florida; Jim Hardie, Sports Department, *Miami Herald,* Miami, Florida; Mary Hasselgrave, West Orange, New Jersey; Jim Henry, Mad River Canoes, Waitsfield, Vermont; Robert Jansenius, Panama City Beach, Florida; Paul and Riva Leviten, Big G Food Markets, Pawtucket, Rhode Island; Roger McGregor, Alumacraft Boat Co., St. Peter, Minnesota; Ron Mason, John B. Anderson & Associates, Denver, Colorado; Michael Matlack, Matlack Yacht Builders, Inc., Stuart, Florida; Walter N. Meloon, vice president, Correct Craft, Orlando, Florida; Keith Menzie, Plantation, Florida; Alan Miller, Fair Lawn, New Jersey; Ray Miller, Program Specialist, Small Craft, American National Red Cross; Joseph Moore, Juno Isles, Florida; Richard Moore, Richmond, Texas; Audie Morton, Hollywood, Florida; Jane Pegel, Williams Bay, Wisconsin; Pete Perdue, Ocean Reef Club, Upper Key Largo, Florida; Dr. Harry M. Price, Libertyville, Illinois; Bill Riviere, North Berwick, Maine; Harry Roberts, editor, *Wilderness Camping,* Schenectady, New York; Dwight Rockwell, Rockwell & Newell, New York City; Emil Rybovich, Rybovich Boat Yard, West Palm Beach, Florida; John Rybovich, Rybovich Boat Yard, West Palm Beach, Florida; Don Rypinski, Newport Beach, California; Hoyle Schweitzer, Windsurfer International, Marina Del Ray, California; Harold Sharp, Bass Anglers Sportsman Society of America, Montgomery, Alabama; Dieter Stiller, Hans Klepper Corp., New York City; E. H. "Bud" Swenson, Jr., Pompano Beach, Florida; Eric Swenson, Pompano Beach, Florida; Paul Treydte, Quik-N-Easy Products, Monrovia, California; William K. Verner, Adirondack Museum, Blue Mountain Lake, New York; Rod Webb, Evinrude Motors, Milwaukee, Wisconsin.

Picture Credits   *Credits from left to right are separated by semicolons, from top to bottom by dashes.*

Cover—Stephen Green-Armytage. 6,7—Steve Wilkings. 9—Guy de la Valdene. 12—Stephen Green-Armytage. 14,15—Bill Browning; courtesy Grumman Boats—R. V. Fuschetto from Photo Researchers; Bill Browning (2). 16—Courtesy Boston Whaler. 17 through 40—Stephen Green-Armytage. 42,43—Boats drawn by Dale Gustafson; drawings by Fred Wolff (2). 44 through 47—Drawings by Fred Wolff. 48,49—Boats drawn by Dale Gustafson; drawings by Fred Wolff; courtesy U.S. Geological Survey. 50 through 55—Drawings by Dale Gustafson. 56,57—Drawings by Peter McGinn. 58,59—Drawings by Dale Gustafson. 60,61—Drawings by Dale Gustafson; map and drawing by Fred Wolff. 62,63—Drawings by Peter McGinn. 64,65—Drawings by Fred Wolff. 66 through 75—Drawings by Dale Gustafson. 76,77—Drawings by Peter McGinn. 78—Courtesy B.A.S.S.; Stephen Green-Armytage for SPORTS ILLUSTRATED. 79 through 85—Stephen Green-Armytage for SPORTS ILLUSTRATED. 86—Clyde H. Smith. 88,89—Drawings by Dale Gustafson. 90—Drawing by Dale Gustafson—courtesy Minnesota Historical Society. 91,92, 93—Drawings by Dale Gustafson. 94 through 99—Drawings by Peter McGinn. 100 through 103—Drawings by Fred Wolff. 104 through 107—Jim Olive. 108, 109—Bob Gomel from TIME-LIFE Picture Agency. 110—Mark Hatlee. 111—Mark Hatlee—John Urban. 112—Courtesy Old Town Canoe Company. 113—Drawing by Peter McGinn—Mark Hatlee. 114—Del Mulkey for SPORTS ILLUSTRATED. 115—Drawing by Fred Wolff—John Urban. 116 through 119—John Blaustein. 120,121—Seneca Ray Stoddard, courtesy Maitland DeSormo, Adirondack Yesteryears. 122,123—Seneca Ray Stoddard, courtesy Maitland DeSormo, Adirondack Yesteryears; Seneca Ray Stoddard, courtesy Adirondack Museum—Seneca Ray Stoddard, courtesy Adirondack Museum; Seneca Ray Stoddard, courtesy Maitland DeSormo, Adirondack Yesteryears. 124, 125—Seneca Ray Stoddard, courtesy Maitland DeSormo, Adirondack Yesteryears, except bottom right Seneca Ray Stoddard, courtesy Adirondack Museum. 126,127—Seneca Ray Stoddard, courtesy Maitland DeSormo, Adirondack Yesteryears. 128—Michael Philip Manheim. 130,131—Drawings by Whitman Studio, Inc. 132,133—Drawings by Peter McGinn. 134 through 137—Drawings by Whitman Studio, Inc. 138,139—William Decker from Photophile, San Diego—drawing by Whitman Studio, Inc.; Michael Philip Manheim from Photo Researchers. 140—Michael Philip Manheim from Photo Researchers—drawing by Whitman Studio, Inc. 141—Michael Philip Manheim from Photo Researchers. 142,143—Drawings by Whitman Studio, Inc.; Tom McCarthy. 144—Tom Sawyer. 146—Steve Wilkings. 147—Drawings by Dale Gustafson. 148,149—Steve Wilkings. 150, 151—Eric Schweikardt for SPORTS ILLUSTRATED; Steve Wilkings. 152,153—Tom McCarthy; drawings by Dale Gustafson. 154,155—Alfred Levy. 156,157—Eric Schweikardt. 158,159—Henry Bossett; Alfred Levy—courtesy Snowbird Fun Products; Eric Schweikardt (2). 160 through 167—Eric Schweikardt, drawings by Dale Gustafson.

Index
Page numbers in italics indicate a photograph or drawing of the subject mentioned.